The Space Economy at a Glance 2011

This work is published on the responsibility of the Secretary-General of the OECD. The opinions expressed and arguments employed herein do not necessarily reflect the official views of the Organisation or of the governments of its member countries.

Please cite this publication as:
OECD (2011), *The Space Economy at a Glance 2011*, OECD Publishing.
http://dx.doi.org/10.1787/9789264111790-en

ISBN 978-92-64-08464-3 (print)
ISBN 978-92-64-11179-0 (PDF)
ISBN 978-92-64-11356-5 (HTML)

The statistical data for Israel are supplied by and under the responsibility of the relevant Israeli authorities. The use of such data by the OECD is without prejudice to the status of the Golan Heights, East Jerusalem and Israeli settlements in the West Bank under the terms of international law.

Photo credits: Cover © Stocktrek/Corbis
Chapter II: © Colin Anderson/Blend Images/Getty Images
Chapter III: © Stuart Gregory/Photodisc/Getty Images
Chapter IV: © Tetraimages/Inmagine
Chapter V: © Stockbyte/Getty Images
Chapter VI: © Shutterstock/MC_PP.

Corrigenda to OECD publications may be found on line at: *www.oecd.org/publishing/corrigenda*.
© OECD 2011

You can copy, download or print OECD content for your own use, and you can include excerpts from OECD publications, databases and multimedia products in your own documents, presentations, blogs, websites and teaching materials, provided that suitable acknowledgment of OECD as source and copyright owner is given. All requests for public or commercial use and translation rights should be submitted to *rights@oecd.org*. Requests for permission to photocopy portions of this material for public or commercial use shall be addressed directly to the Copyright Clearance Center (CCC) at *info@copyright.com* or the Centre français d'exploitation du droit de copie (CFC) at *contact@cfcopies.com*.

Foreword

The Space Economy at a Glance (2011) provides a statistical overview of the global space sector and its contributions to economic activity. This publication is an updated, more comprehensive version of The Space Economy at a Glance (2007), the first-ever OECD statistical overview of the emerging space economy. The new edition provides not only recent indicators and statistics based on both official and private data, but also a strategic outlook that identifies key issues for the future. The figures cover many countries, and, for first the time, include various official statistics concerning the Indian and Chinese space programmes.

The publication is the result of several years of co-operative efforts with the space community. In 2002, the OECD's strategic foresight unit (the International Futures Programme, IFP) launched a project to explore how space technologies could contribute to finding solutions to some of the major challenges facing society. Two publications resulted from that in-depth project. Space 2030: The Future of Space Applications (OECD, 2004) explored promising space applications for the 21st century. Space 2030: Tackling Society's Challenges (OECD, 2005) assessed the strengths and weaknesses of the regulatory frameworks that govern space, and formulated a policy framework that OECD governments might use to ensure fullest possible realisation of the potential offered by space. In particular, it identified space infrastructure as a key issue for the future development of the space economy.

The space sector plays an increasingly pivotal role in the efficient functioning of modern societies and their economic development. The use of satellite technology in navigation, communications, meteorology, and earth observation is giving rise to a growing stream of applications in such areas as air traffic control, transport, natural resource management, agriculture, environmental and climate change monitoring, entertainment and so on, which in turn are creating new downstream uses and new markets. Space is increasingly seen as an important potential source of economic growth, social wellbeing and sustainable development.

Upon completion of the two-year OECD space project, there was strong encouragement from a number of institutions, especially space-related agencies, for the OECD IFP to continue exploring the economic dimensions of space infrastructure. The year 2006 saw the launch of the OECD Forum on Space Economics (the "Space Forum"), an innovative platform for international dialogue on the social and economic aspects of space activities. This Forum is supported by contributions and/or expertise from a number of governments and space agencies: ASI (Agenzia Spaziale Italiana, the Italian Space Agency), the UK Space Agency, CNES (Centre National d'Études Spatiales, the French Space Agency), CSA (Canadian Space Agency), ESA (European Space Agency), NASA (National Aeronautics and Space Administration), Norwegian Space Centre (Norsk Romsenter) and USGS (United States Geological Survey). One of the Forum's first outputs was The Space Economy at a Glance in 2007. Other outputs have included case studies examining the socio-economic contributions of space applications. The first publication of these studies, Space Technologies and Climate Change (2008), looked at the role of these technologies in tackling some of the major problems posed by climate change, focusing on examples from water management, marine resources and maritime transport. A second, upcoming case study publication, Space Technologies and Global Food

Supplies (2011), will look at how space applications could assess food stocks via remote sensing, or could render the food transport industry more cost-efficient and environment-friendly through navigation aids.

This publication was prepared by Claire Jolly, Policy Analyst in the OECD International Futures Programme (IFP), under the direction and guidance of Barrie Stevens, Head of IFP and Pierre Alain Schieb, Head of Futures Projects. Anita Gibson provided editorial and administrative assistance. Logan Gibson and Hyungsoo Woo conducted research and analysis. The team benefited from contributions from colleagues inside the Organisation, particularly Hélène Dernis from the Directorate for Science, Technology and Industry (STI) for patents.

We particularly thank the members of the Space Forum for providing data and valuable comments. Experts from other organisations also kindly contributed to this work: industry representatives in North America and Europe, who provided figures for selected sections on space applications (telecommunications, earth observation, navigation); experts in industry associations who provided original data and suggestions, particularly Pierre Lionnet, senior economist at Eurospace and Norihiro Sakamoto from the Society of Japanese Aerospace Companies; Radhika Ramachandran from the Indian Space Research Organisation (ISRO) who helped with our Indian statistics; Ken Davidian from the FAA who provided ideas for tackling the "new space" industry; and finally Agata Szydelko from NATO with information on satellite bandwidth. Our gratitude goes to all the organisations and individuals who contributed to this publication.

Table of Contents

Acronyms 7

Executive Summary 9

Introduction 13

I. The Space Sector in 2011 and Beyond 19
    1. A new world map of space powers 20
    2. The space economy as an engine of economic growth 27
    3. Preserving a skilled workforce in the space sector 34
    4. New technologies and innovative applications on the horizon 41
    References 45

II. Readiness Factors: Inputs to the Space Economy 49
    1. Governmental budgets for space activities 50
    2. Capital stocks: Space assets in orbit and on the ground 54
    3. Human capital 56

III. Intensity: Activities and Outputs in the Space Economy 59
    4. The manufacturing space industry 60
    5. The satellite telecommunications sector 62
    6. The satellite earth observation sector 64
    7. Insurance market for space activities 66
    8. International trade in selected space products 68
    9. Innovation for future economic growth: Patents 70
    10. Space launch activities worldwide 72
    11. Space exploration activities 74

IV. Impacts: Bringing Space Down to Earth 77
    12. Defining socio-economic impacts from space programmes 78
    13. Indirect industrial effects 80
    14. Economic growth (regional, national) 82
    15. Efficiency/productivity gains 84

V. National Spotlights on Selected Countries 87
    16. United States 88
    17. France 90
    18. Italy 92
    19. Canada 94
    20. United Kingdom 96

21. Norway	98
22. India	100
23. China	102
24. Brazil	104

VI. The Global Aerospace Sector in Perspective 107

25. Production and value-added	108
26. Research and development	110
27. Trade	112

This book has...

StatLinks

A service that delivers Excel® files from the printed page!

Look for the StatLinks at the bottom right-hand corner of the tables or graphs in this book. To download the matching Excel® spreadsheet, just type the link into your Internet browser, starting with the *http://dx.doi.org* prefix.
If you're reading the PDF e-book edition, and your PC is connected to the Internet, simply click on the link. You'll find StatLinks appearing in more OECD books.

Acronyms

AEB	Agência Espacial Brasileira (Brazilian Space Agency)
AIA	Aerospace Industries Association
AIAC	Aerospace Industries Association of Canada
AIAD	Associazione Industrie per l'Aerospazio i sistemi e la Difesa (Italian Industries Association for Aerospace Systems and Defence)
AIS	Automatic Identification System
ASAS	Associazione per I Servizi, le Applicazioni e le Tecnologie ICT per lo Spazio (Italian Association for Space-based Applications and Services)
ASI	Agenzia Spaziale Italiana (Italian Space Agency)
BERD	Business Enterprise Research and Development
BNSC	British National Space Centre
BRIC	Brazil, the Russian Federation, India and China
BRIIC	Brazil, the Russian Federation, India, Indonesia and China
CAST	China Aerospace Science and Technology Group
CDTI	Centro Para el Desarrollo Tecnológico Industrial (Spain)
CEOS	Committee on Earth Observation Satellites
CHELEM	Comptes Harmonisés sur les Échanges et L'Économie Mondiale
CNES	Centre National d'Études Spatiales (French Space Agency)
CONAE	Comisión Nacional de Actividades Espaciales (Argentine)
CRESDA	Center for Resource Satellite Data and Applications (China)
CSA	Canadian Space Agency
CSIRO	Commonwealth Scientific and Industrial Research Organisation (Australia)
DBS	Direct Broadcasting Datellite
DLR	Deutsches Zentrum für Luft- und Raumfahrt (German Aerospace Center)
DTH	Direct-to-Home Satellite
EC	European Commission
EPO	European Patent Office
ESA	European Space Agency
FAA	Federal Aviation Administration
FDI	Foreign Direct Investment
FSS	Fixed Satellite Service
FTE	Full-time equivalent
GBAORD	Government Budget Appropriations or Outlays for Research and Development
GIFAS	Groupement des Industries Françaises Aéronautiques et Spatiales
GISTDA	Geo-Informatics and Space Technology Development Agency (Thailand)
GPS	Global Positioning System
HRST	Human Resources in Science and Technology
IFP	International Futures Programme
INPE	Instituto Nacional de Pesquisas Espaciais (Brazil)

INSEE		Institut National de la Statistique et des Études Économiques
ISRO		Indian Space Research Organisation
ITAR		International Traffic in Arms Regulations
ITCS		International Trade in Commodity Statistics
ITU		International Telecommunications Union
JAXA		Japanese Aerospace Exploration Agency
KARI		Korean Aerospace Research institute
MSS		Mobile Satellite Service
NAICS		North American Industry Classification System
NASA		National Aeronautics and Space Administration
NOAA		National Oceanic and Atmospheric Administration
NRSCC		National Remote Sensing Center of China
NSAU		National Space Agency of Ukraine
NSC		Norwegian Space Centre
OECD		Organisation for Economic Co-operation and Development
PCT		Patent Co-operation Treaty
PPP		Purchase Power Parities
Roscosmos		Russian Federal Space Agency
SANSA		South African National Space Agency
SJAC		Society of Japanese Aerospace Companies
SME		Small and medium enterprises
SNA		System of National Accounts
SNSB		Swedish National Space Board
SSA		Space Situational Awareness
UKSA		United Kingdom Space Agency
USGS		United States Geological Survey
USPTO		United States Patent and Trademark Office

Executive Summary

Space technologies have become an important part of everyday life. Weather forecasting, air traffic control, global communications and broadcasting – these and many other essential activities would be almost unthinkable today without satellite technology.

A new international landscape for space activities...

The landscape for space activities is starting to change radically. It now includes a wide diversity of institutional and private actors. There have never been so many countries with satellites in orbit (more than 50 countries). The emergence of Brazil, India and China as established space powers alongside the Russian Federation (i.e. the BRIC countries), but also as a new nexus of space technology transfers towards developing economies, is a key characteristic of the new landscape. The Russian Federation has for instance launched more rockets than any other country every year since 2006. Asian countries led by China (15 launches in 2010, like the United States) are also gradually outdistancing Europe in terms of the number of launches and satellites sent in orbit.

The total space budget of the 35 countries examined in this report represents conservatively USD 64.4 billion in 2009, and an estimated USD 65.3 billion in 2010, with the bulk of funding in G7 and BRIC countries. All G20 countries have space programmes. Five countries have invested more than USD 2 billion in both 2009 and 2010 (the United States, China, Japan, France and the Russian Federation), with the United States leading the way at more than USD 43 billion. As countries have diverse strategies in developing space programmes (i.e. focusing on manufacturing or selected downstream activities), special spotlight sections have been drafted in this report on current members of the OECD Forum on Space Economics (the United States, France, Italy, Canada, the United Kingdom, Norway), as well as on India, China and Brazil.

Almost 1 000 operational satellites are now in orbit with diverse earth observation, telecommunications, navigation and positioning missions. In parallel to the growing importance of these down-to-earth applications, science and space exploration remain key missions of space agencies, invigorating international scientific co-operation. In early 2011, seven probes are flying through the solar system, three satellites are orbiting Mars, two active rovers are on Mars' surface, and two satellites are orbiting Venus. In the 2009-10 period, China, India, Japan, Europe and the United States each launched a spacecraft to orbit the Moon. China has already launched several taikonauts in earth's orbit, while the International Space Station has been inhabited and visited by astronauts and cosmonauts since 2003.

EXECUTIVE SUMMARY

... the space economy as an engine of economy growth...

In comparison to other sectors, the space sector has fared relatively well since 2008 despite the economic crisis, thanks to its specificities as a key strategic sector (*i.e.* national imperatives and institutional research and development funding), but also because of the vibrant "space economy". This space economy includes many commercial activities that have been derived over the years from the space sector's research and development (R&D) missions. Several mature downstream activities have reached mass markets, and include information technology products and services, such as satellite television and GPS receivers. Even tourism-related packages are starting to be commercialised (*e.g.* space-related amusement parks, suborbital flights):

- Mapping the space economy remains a complex process. Estimates vary widely, and many involve some degree of double counting. But the most reliable estimates suggest that the revenues derived from the wide diversity of space-related products and services amounted to some USD 150-165 billion in 2009.
- Telecommunications still represent the main commercial space market, and several satellite operators have broken records in revenues since 2008 despite the economic crisis. They have benefited from growing mass markets (satellite television broadcasting) and a robust demand from institutional users (defence, new customers in the developing world, development of anchor contracts). The lease of transponders and communications via satellite represented some USD 11-15 billion in revenues, while satellite broadcasting (*e.g.* television via satellite) some USD 65-72 billion in 2009.
- The geopositioning market, a growing new segment building on satellite capacities (with products such as the now common car-navigation), represents USD 15 billion in revenue in 2009. With the advances in smartphones and other mobile products, all offering geopositioning capabilities, more growth is expected.
- Other sectors include the satellite earth observation sector, a market valued in 2009 at some USD 900 million to USD 1.2 billion, and the space insurance industry, which generates around USD 750-800 million a year.
- The overall growth of space applications has impacted the rest of the value chain, particularly the main satellite manufacturers. The commercial and institutional demand for satellites remains relatively strong and geographically diversified, particularly for military/dual-use satellites. The total five-year value of satellite production is estimated at some USD 65.5 billion.

This overall encouraging environment for the space sector, in the midst of a serious economic crisis, may not last indefinitely. On the commercial front, despite the growth of space applications and the financial success of satellite telecommunications, the main operators will reach the end of a cycle over the next three years, having placed all the contracts for replenishing their respective fleets of satellites. But more importantly, the space sector manufacturers are still dependent worldwide on institutional budgets for much of the R&D and on governmental customers for satellites and launchers. The potential restrictions in budgets in many countries, in science and defence particularly, may affect the industry over the next three years, as budget cuts filter down the entire value chain.

... more innovation for future economic growth...

The space sector has often been considered one of the main frontrunners of technological development, since the beginning of the space age. The number of space-related patents has almost quadrupled in fifteen years. The countries' share in space-related patents over the 2000-08 period shows the United States and Europe leading, followed by Korea and Japan. However, in terms of revealed technological advantage, several countries demonstrate a level of specialisation in space technologies patenting, particularly the Russian Federation, France, Israel and the United States.

Over the next five years, many advances are expected in the classical sphere of space applications (telecommunications and navigation applications), where satellites could contribute further to the development of commercial information systems and networks (*e.g.* more broadband to rural areas, high definition and 3D television via satellite, air traffic management). But in addition, several relatively new space systems could be moving from demonstrations to potentially routine systems. They include automatic identification systems (AIS) via satellite which allow countries to monitor ship traffic along their coasts, and space situational awareness, which serves to track the trajectories of operational satellites and large space debris in orbit.

... space activities and returns on investments...

The investments in space programmes are often justified by the scientific, technological, industrial and security capabilities they bring. But these investments can also provide interesting socio-economic returns such as increased industrial activity, and bring cost efficiencies and productivity gains to other fields (*e.g.* weather forecasting, telemedicine, environmental monitoring and agriculture previsions):

- In a majority of countries, space programmes are contracted out to national industry. Although economic impacts may vary depending on the country and the level of its specialisation (*e.g.* applications *versus* manufacturing), records on positive industrial returns from institutional investments are growing. Norway, which has a small but active space programme, has detected a positive multiplier effect since the 1990s, *i.e.* for each million Norwegian kroner of governmental support through the European Space Agency (ESA) or national support programmes, the Norwegian space sector companies have on the average attained an additional turnover, usually as new exports or new activities outside the space sector. In 2009, NOK 1 million invested provided a return of some 4.7 million. In Denmark too, each EUR million of Danish contributions to the European Space Agency (ESA) has generated a turnover of EUR 3.7 million in average. In Belgium, the same type of multiplier has been detected, for each EUR million of governmental support through ESA, EUR 1.4 million have been generated by the Belgian industry. In the United Kingdom, the space industry's value-added multiplier has been estimated to be 1.91. Finally, the most recent Federal Aviation Administration (FAA) study on the economic impacts of the US commercial space activities has also shown a rather stable multiplier ratio since 2002. In 2009, for every dollar spent commercial space transportation industry, USD 4.9 resulted in indirect and induced economic impact.

- Earth observation data and geopositioning products are benefitting to an increasingly large number of sectors, via cost efficiencies and productivity gains. Weather prediction, which relies particularly on meteorological satellites coverage, has become a routine service for citizens, companies and governments alike. In economic terms, a recent study in the United States has estimated that the benefit of the investment in public weather forecasts and warnings represents annually about USD 31.5 billion, compared to the USD 5.1 billion cost of generating the information. Adequate irrigation is also essential to improve food productivity in many regions, especially as water is becoming scarcer. In India, under the "Rajiv Gandhi National Drinking Water Mission" of the Ministry of Rural Development, Indian satellite remote sensing technology is already used for preparing groundwater maps in ten states. Since the success rate of bore wells reached already around 90% in these states, the project was extended to cover the entire country.

… preserving a skilled workforce in the space sector…

The space economy with all its various downstream products and services contributes to employ hundreds of thousands of employees in diverse OECD and non-OECD countries, although data are not known for all countries. Focussing on the narrower space manufacturing sector, some 170 000 people work in the space industry in the United States, some 31 000 people in Europe and 50 000 in China. The space sector is generally a very concentrated industry, as for example, four large industrial holdings are directly responsible for more than 70% of total European space industry employment. The dominant job categories comprise engineers and technicians involved in designing, manufacturing and operating space and ground segments, but also information technology specialists.

As in other parts of the economy, the space sector is particularly affected by the large wave of retirement of the baby boom generation. Many of the engineers and scientists who have developed space systems over the past three decades are retiring, and this situation comes in a context of a sharp decrease in the engineering and scientific population under 30 years old in most OECD countries. Although space remains *a priori* a very attractive field for young students, the space sector increasingly competes with other sectors for the scientifically minded students (*e.g.* game software development, biotechnologies). Taking into account the increased globalisation of the space industry and emergence of many talents in new space-faring countries, the international mobility of human resources in science and technology could become a key feature in the space industry employment strategies, although national security restrictions would still often apply (*i.e.* civilian-military nature of many space systems).

… outlook for the space economy…

Societal challenges – such as the environment, the use of natural resources, the increasing mobility of people and goods, growing security threats, and the move towards the information society – are intensifying in both OECD and non-OECD countries. In parallel, a number of countries are rapidly emerging as new actors in the world's economy.

Some countries may see their institutional space budgets suffer from potential negative effects, caused by near-term economic conditions. But overall the globalisation of space activities, as well as the practical contributions of space applications to meet key societal challenges, are so significant that the space sector and the wider space economy could probably continue expanding for the foreseeable future.

Introduction

The Space Economy at a Glance provides a quantitative, internationally comparable view of not only the space sector itself, but also its broader role in the economy and society. This 2011 edition brings together published and unpublished data and statistics from official and unofficial sources, as well as from OECD databases that cover a wide range of space applications, public space budgets, space sector revenues, trade in space products and space patents to name but a few, in order to illustrate the economic and societal impacts of space-based activities.

Defining the space economy

Space technologies are increasingly an important part of everyday life. Weather forecasting, air traffic control, global communications and broadcasting – these and many other essential activities would be almost unthinkable today without satellite technology. But despite the growing number of countries developing space systems and applications, internationally agreed definitions for statistical terminology on space activities do not yet exist.

The space sector. According to OECD classifications, there are nine main product groups of high-technology: 1) aerospace; 2) computers and office machines; 3) electronics and telecommunications; 4) pharmacy; 5) scientific instruments; 6) electrical machinery; 7) chemistry; 8) non-electrical machinery; and 9) armaments (Hatzichronoglou, 1997). The space sector is embedded into these wider high-tech sectors, mainly in aerospace, with segments in electronics and telecommunications and even armaments, since rockets are considered as weapons (*i.e.* missiles) in most countries (OECD, 2007).

The current edition of the United Nations International Standard Industrial Classification (ISIC Rev. 4 released in August 2008) includes most parts of the space sector under different aggregate categories. There is no specific "space activity" classification in the ISIC, and disentangling the space sector from the larger aerospace and defence sectors remains a challenge in most countries. This is also true for other international classifications, such as the Central Product Classification (Version 2) or the Harmonised Commodity Description and Coding System (HS) of the World Customs Organization (OECD, 2011).

At national and regional levels, some countries go further in identifying space products and services as economic activities, by adding more digits to the general international codes. But this causes discrepancies when trying to compare the data internationally. This classification problem, often found for emerging economic sectors, is however not new. Already in the late 1960s, at the beginning of the space age, the general "missiles and spacecraft" statistical category was identified as causing methodological difficulties in the United States when trying to assess aerospace prices over time because of the heterogeneity of the products covered in the single category (Campbell, 1970).

One interim solution is to build on existing codes to advance international comparability. This could be done by encouraging statistical rapprochement between selected countries, using the same lower digits codes and definitions, and gathering data via common industry surveys using the same key questions. Such efforts could be spearheaded by the private sector, particularly via aerospace industry associations agreeing on a number of key definitions. Co-operation in that area is increasing via the OECD Space Forum's activities, for example via the regular meetings of "the space economy" technical committee. This committee was created in 2008 with the International Astronautical Federation to tackle the issue of comparability of economic data on the space sector. Ultimately, a move to change international classifications for an increasing number of space activities could contribute to more clarity. This already occurred during the ISIC Rev. 4, which created a new and separate ISIC Class specifically for satellite telecommunications activities.

The wider space economy. Trying to better identify statistically the different space applications has thus become an important theme, as the space sector has been spurring more commercial activities outside its traditional research and development (R&D) scope over the years. Activities include specific information technology products and services, such as GPS receivers, satellite television and even investments in new tourism-related activities (*e.g.* space-related amusement parks, suborbital flights).

This wider "space economy" can be defined using different angles. It can be defined by its products (*e.g.* satellites, launchers…), by its services (*e.g.* broadcasting, imagery/data delivering…), by its programmatic objectives (*e.g.* military, robotic space exploration, human spaceflight, earth observation, telecommunications…), by its actors/value chains (from R&D actors to users), and by its impacts (*e.g.* direct and indirect benefits). One drawback is that narrow definitions might ignore important aspects, such as the R&D actors (*e.g.* labs and universities), the role of the military (*i.e.* as investor in R&D budgets and a customer for space services), or ignore scientific and space exploration programmes altogether.

The OECD Space Forum members established that the space economy should not be limited to only a few characteristics because of the growing pervasiveness of space applications in many daily activities (meteorology, telecommunications…). Using lessons learned from other sectors (the information society notably), a broad definition of the space economy seemed appropriate to encompass the different dimensions of programmes, services, actors. The proposed working definition below represents the starting point of this publication:

The space economy is the full range of activities and the use of resources that create and provide value and benefits to human beings in the course of exploring, understanding, managing and utilising space. Hence, it includes all public and private actors involved in developing, providing and using space-related products and services, ranging from research and development, the manufacture and use of space infrastructure (ground stations, launch vehicles and satellites) to space-enabled applications (navigation equipment, satellite phones, meteorological services, etc.) and the scientific knowledge generated by such activities. It follows that the space economy goes well beyond the space sector itself, since it also comprises the increasingly pervasive and continually changing impacts (both quantitative and qualitative) of space-derived products, services and knowledge on economy and society.

Thus, the space economy is larger than the traditional space sector (*e.g.* rockets and satellites) and it involves more and more new services and product providers (*e.g.* geographic information systems developers, navigation equipment sellers) who are using space systems' capacities to create new products. However the unique capabilities

Figure 0.1. **The space economy's simplified value chain**

| Space actors (Institutional R&D, industry and services providers) | ⟷ | Non-space actors |

- R&D centres
- Laboratories
- Universities
- Manufacturers
- Satellites
- Launchers
- Ground segment
- Operators
- Digital data providers
- Satellite signal providers
- Information services providers
- Value adders/integrators
- Retail delivery
- Ground equipment/devices developers

offered by satellites (i.e. ubiquitous data, communications links, imagery…) represent often only small, albeit essential, components of those new products and services (see Figure 0.1).

As a consequence, the space economy concept helps capture the space sector's derived products and services. But one should be careful not to extend this concept so wide as to lose the space "link" and risk overselling the space sector's socio-economic impacts. As the space economy overlaps with many fields, more methodological work is ongoing to illustrate in greater detail space economy-related services.

What is new in the publication?

This publication is an updated and more comprehensive version of *The Space Economy at a Glance* (2007), the first OECD statistical overview of the emerging space economy. This version provides not only new indicators and statistics, featuring both official and private data, but also a strategic outlook for the space sector, identifying key issues for the future. The new items featured in this publication include:

- *More data sources*. More official sources are collected in this edition, with more OECD calculations to facilitate international comparisons when possible.
- *Wider geographical coverage*. The figures cover many countries, and for first time include official statistics and new OECD calculations concerning the Brazilian, Indian, Israeli and Chinese space programmes.
- *More topics*. Key issues for decision makers and analysts are covered in this edition: the role of the space sector as a potential source of economic growth; the evolutions of a skilled workforce in such a high-tech sector; the impacts of international technology transfers, particularly between OECD and Brazil, the Russian Federation, India and China (i.e. the BRIC countries); and the role of military space.
- *Methodological tools*. In addition to new figures that have been integrated into the publication to facilitate analysis, an OECD Working Paper is being published as a *Guide to Measuring the Space Economy at a Glance*. This paper provides readers and analysts with more information on methodological issues concerning indicators on the space sector (e.g. discussions on industrial classifications).

Structure of the publication

The publication features a strategic outlook for the space sector, identifies key issues for the future and provides statistics and indicators on the space economy. The data based on official and private sources are presented in a framework that consists of three stages: readiness (inputs), intensity (outputs) and impacts. Each stage provides an indication of the maturity of the sector. The diagram below illustrates the different steps from readiness to impacts.

Figure 0.2. **The different phases of development of the space economy**

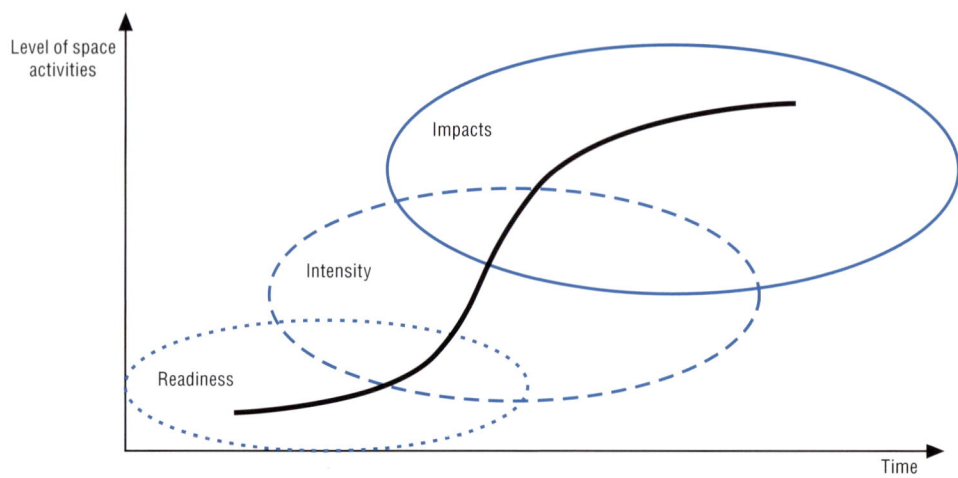

The publication consists of six chapters:

1. The first chapter of the publication provides a prospective view of the space sector, featuring some key issues that will shape its future. It includes: the growth and impacts of international technology transfers in mapping a new world of space powers; the role of commercial actors; the evolution of a skilled workforce in the space sector; and the development of new technologies and innovative applications on the horizon.

2. The readiness factors (inputs) of the space economy consist of the overall technical, commercial, human capital and financial infrastructures necessary to engage in pertinent space activities. This chapter deals with the financial and human resources that are employed in producing space-related hardware and the provision of relevant services. It examines R&D, financial support for space programmes and human capital.

3. The intensity factors (outputs) of the space economy describe the use that is made of space activities. The outputs refer to the specific space-related outcomes that are derived from the inputs. Thus, outputs may include products or services that are produced or provided in the realm of the space sector, such as the number of space launches or the number of space exploration missions. They also include the benefits to industries/nations, including financial benefits (sales and trade revenues) and indications of future financial benefits (i.e. patents).

4. The impacts of the space economy, which are difficult to measure, consist of the "societal value-added" created by space activities. Examples provided are of benefit to society as a whole, but also cost efficiencies derived from space products and services.

5. The spotlights on selected countries offer some insights into the space-related activities of member countries participating in the OECD Forum on Space Economics and other countries. Data come from their official sources (such as national space agencies or statistical offices) as well as private sources. In this section, direct comparisons between countries are not always possible due to definitional, conceptual and methodical differences.

6. The final chapter on the aerospace sector provides the wider context from which the space economy has emerged. It also highlights the importance of future endeavours to separate the aircraft and spacecraft industry components for more meaningful official data.

Data sources

The Space Economy at a Glance builds on both official and private sector statistics:

- OECD databases and reports, which provide the most international comparability;
- official statistics, which consist of data from national statistical offices, national space agencies and other governmental departments; and
- private data sources, which include industry associations and consulting firms.

The quality of available measures and comparable data for the space economy varies strongly for the input, output and impact stages. Some official statistical data are available for the readiness (input) factors (although not always readily comparable) and the intensity (output) factors, but these need to be supplemented by private data sources (*e.g.* industry surveys for revenues of the space sector). There are relatively less data on impacts, although the number and quality of datasets have improved since the early 2000s, as more countries study the impacts of their respective space sector on the wider economy. In order to provide a better indication of the state of the space economy, more work on the concepts and definitions for the space sector and the larger space economy is needed. This calls for significant international co-operation, and the OECD Forum on Space Economics is working with the space community to provide a platform for such work.

References

Campbell, H.G. (1970), *Aerospace Price Indexes*, RAND Corporation, Report prepared for the US Air Force, Washington DC, December.

Hatzichronoglou, T. (1997), "Revision of the High Technology Sector and Product Classification", *OECD Science, Technology and Industry Working Papers*, OECD Publishing, 1997/2, Paris.

OECD (2007), *The Space Economy at a Glance 2007*, OECD Publishing, Paris.

OECD (2011), "Measuring the Space Economy: A Guide", OECD Publishing, Paris (forthcoming).

Chapter I

The Space Sector in 2011 and Beyond

> *The geopolitical landscape of the world has considerably changed in two decades and this can also be seen in the strategic space sector. This first chapter features some key issues that could shape the future of the sector including: the emergence of a new world map of space powers, the growing role of commercial actors, the evolution of a skilled workforce in the space sector, and the development of new technologies and innovative applications on the horizon.*

I. THE SPACE SECTOR IN 2011 AND BEYOND

1. A new world map of space powers

A new international landscape

The international balance of power has changed significantly in the past two decades. The disintegration of the Soviet Union, the economic rise of a number of Asian countries and the ever growing transfers of technologies, facilitated by the rise of the information society, have all contributed to this new international landscape. In 2011, it is characterised by two main features: an ever larger group of countries with satellite capabilities and the emergence of Brazil, India and China, alongside the Russian Federation (i.e. the BRIC countries), as exporters of space technologies.

Space-faring countries have moved from being a small exclusive club relying on strong defence and aerospace industries, to a larger group of advanced and smaller developing countries with very diverse capabilities. As of early 2011, more than 50 countries have launched satellites, while at least ten other countries intend to have their first satellites in orbit over the next five years (Figure 1.1). Ten countries have so far demonstrated independent orbital launch capabilities, and seven countries (i.e. the United States, the Russian Federation, China, Japan, India, Israel and Iran) and the European Space Agency (ESA) have operational launchers (Jaramillo, 2010). Brazil, Korea and Indonesia aim to develop their own launchers over the next five years.

Figure 1.1. **More than 50 countries with spaceflight capabilities in 2010**
Number of countries which launched satellites (independently or via a third party)

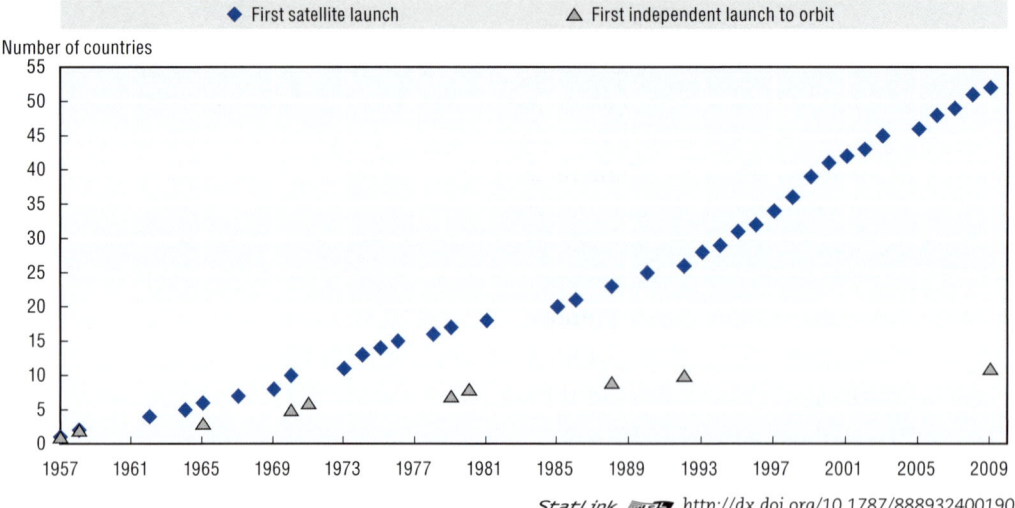

StatLink ⟶ http://dx.doi.org/10.1787/888932400190

Space-faring nations can be regrouped by the number of satellites they have in orbit (Figure 1.2). The United States leads with more than 350 satellites in orbit, followed by the Russian Federation (97 satellites), China (60 satellites) and Japan (40 satellites). A second group of countries with 15-25 satellites in orbit include Canada, France, Germany,

I. THE SPACE SECTOR IN 2011 AND BEYOND

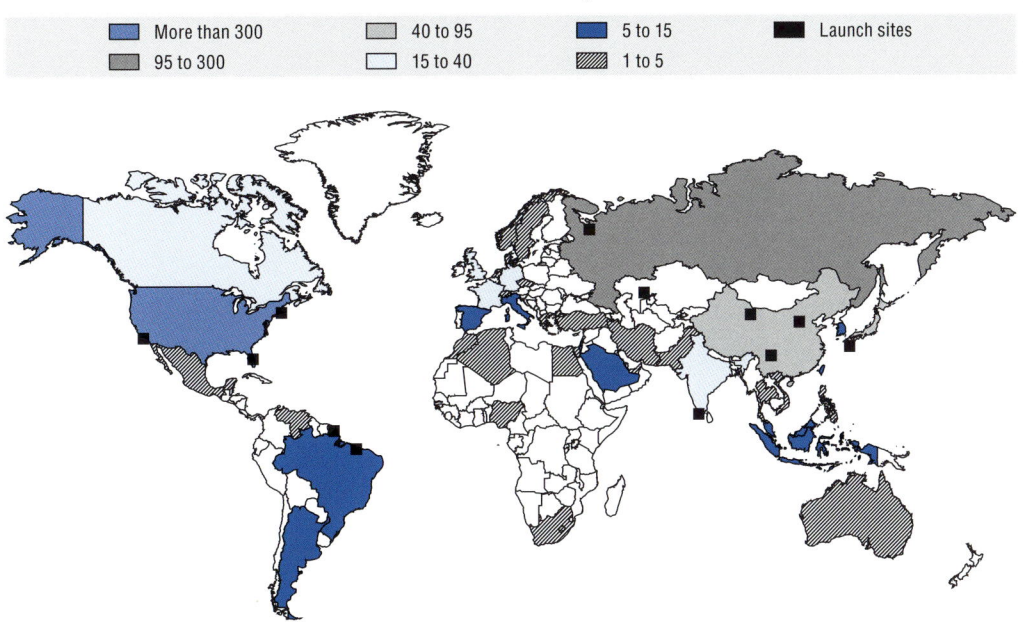

Figure 1.2. **Countries with operational satellites in orbit, 2010**
Number of satellites and main space launch sites

Note: This map is for illustrative purposes and is without prejudice to the status of or sovereignty over any territory covered by this map.

Luxembourg, the United Kingdom and India. They are followed by some 10 countries that have from 5-10 satellites in orbit. The last group is getting larger every year and totals 23 countries in early 2011 with 1-5 operational satellites in orbit.

The emergence of several BRIC countries as established space powers is a second feature of the new international landscape. The Russian Federation was the first country to launch a satellite in orbit in 1957, but it has renewed its commitments to major space-related investments only in the past decade. In the meantime China and India have been heavily investing in space R&D and infrastructure (*e.g.* dedicated space centres), building entire families of indigenous rockets and satellites often through technical co-operation with the Russian Federation. Their share in satellites launched has doubled in one decade (Figure 1.3). In 2006, China became the third country to independently launch humans into space. China's and India's developments in space activities are followed, albeit at a much more moderate rate, by Brazil and Indonesia, although Brazil is currently investing in indigenous launching capabilities. The larger BRIIC grouping which includes Indonesia forms a new nexus of satellite technology transfers to developing countries, thus contributing to the increase in the number of countries with access to space.

The new landscape of space-faring nations is the result of two parallel trends: the ambition of many countries around the world to develop independent national space programmes, and the globalisation of the aerospace and defence industry.

Ambitions to develop national space programmes

The past two decades have seen a sudden increase of new actors entering the space sector. No continent is now excluded, as new space agencies have recently emerged in Asia, Europe, Latin America and Africa. As shown in the Table 1.1, almost all OECD countries have invested in a space programme, even if the funding is often quite modest compared to the largest space actors. The reasons for earmarking some budget resources for space activities can be quite varied (see Chapter IV – concerning the outcomes and

Figure 1.3. **Satellites launched by OECD and BRIIC countries, 1989-98 and 1999-2008**

Satellites funded by public entities (student and university satellites excluded)

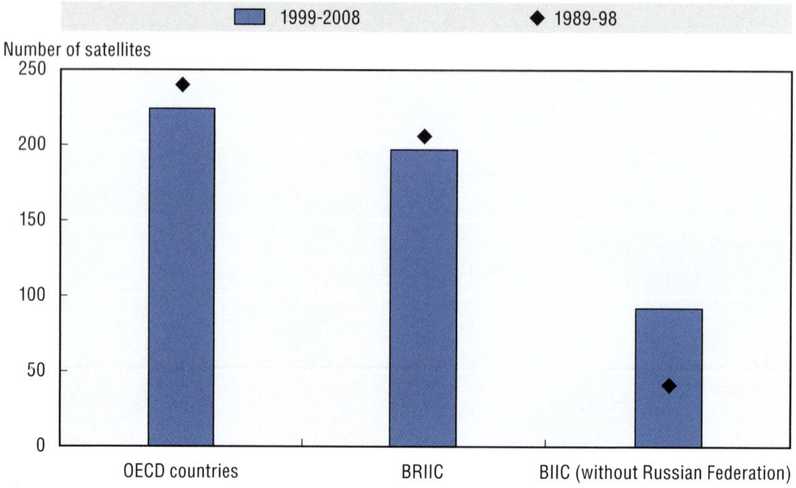

Note: BRIIC countries include Brazil, the Russian Federation, India, Indonesia and China. OECD countries include: Canada, Denmark, France, Germany, Italy, Japan, Korea, Mexico, Norway, Spain, Sweden, Turkey, the United Kingdom, the United States (including also ESA and Eumetsat satellites).

Source: OECD calculations, based on Eurospace (2010).

impacts of space programmes), however there is the general sense that by not having a space programme, even a modest one, a country might be missing out on opportunities and increase dependency on others.

Even in countries with space programmes in existence for decades, new strategies are being established to rationalise and boost existing space efforts. The United Kingdom established a new space agency in April 2010, as a replacement of the interagency British National Space Centre, to improve its national competitiveness and rationalise demand from the public sector. Germany also set up a new space strategy in late 2010, announcing the development of a new space law and increased funding, while Italy's strategic plan for the next decade (2010-20) aims to rebalance funding to initiate new national programmes. Smaller players are also revising their national space strategies to try and participate in more international programmes (*e.g.* Finland with its 2009-11 space plan; Israel with its 2010-15 space plan) (see Box 1.1) or simply develop indigenous capabilities to position themselves to benefit from space applications (*e.g.* Bolivia created a space agency to manage a satellite communications project with Chinese companies; the National Space Agency of South Africa was established as well in late 2010; and several African countries are setting up ground stations to directly receive satellite imagery). A conservative estimate of the space budgets of 35 countries examined represent some USD 65.5 billion in 2010, with the bulk of funding in G7 and BRIC countries.

In parallel to these active national space programmes, bilateral and multilateral co-operation is increasing, as a means to move up the ladder of space technologies, to reduce costs and access to new capabilities. This is not new, but the number of countries developing space-related co-operation is increasing. As an example, although only three countries have the capabilities to launch astronauts to orbit (the Russian Federation, the United States and China), dozens of astronauts from different countries have been able to experience microgravity and conduct experiments over the years. European, Canadian, Indian, Japanese and Brazilian astronauts, to name a few, have all flown to orbit since

Table 1.1. **Key organisations in charge of space programmes in selected OECD countries, 2010**

	Agencies/institutions responsible for space activities[1]
Australia	Space Policy unit, Department of Innovation, Industry, Science and Research.
Austria	Aeronautics and Space Agency (ALR), Austrian Federal Ministry for Transport, Innovation and Technology.
Belgium	Belgian Federal Science Policy Office, Ministry for Economy, Energy, Foreign Trade and Science Policy.
Canada	Canadian Space Agency, Ministry of Industry.
Chile	Chilean Space Agency, Under-Secretariat of Economy of Chile.
Czech Republic	Czech Space Office, Ministry of Education, Youth and Sports.
Denmark	Danish National Space Center, Danish Agency for Science, Technology and Innovation.
Finland	Tekes, Ministry of Trade and Industry.
France	Centre National d'Etudes Spatiales (CNES), Ministry of Education, Research and Technology.
Germany	German Aerospace Centre (DLR), Federal Ministry of Economics and Technology.
Greece	General Secretariat of Research and Technology, Ministry of Development.
Hungary	Hungarian Space Office, Ministry of Informatics and Communications.
Ireland	Enterprise Ireland, Ministry for Enterprise, Trade and Innovation.
Israel	Israel Space Agency, Ministry of Science and Technology.
Italy	Italian Space Agency (ASI), Ministry of University and Research.
Japan	Japan Aerospace Exploration Agency (JAXA), Secretariat of Strategic Headquarters for Space Policy, under the Prime Minister.
Korea	Korea Aerospace Research Institute (KARI), Ministry of education, science and technology.
Luxembourg	Luxinnovation, Ministry of Higher Education and Research.
Mexico	Mexican Space Agency.
Netherlands	Netherlands Space Office, Steering committee regrouping representatives of the Ministry of Economic Affairs, Ministry of Education, Culture and Science, Ministry of Transport, Public Works and Water Management and the Netherlands Organization for Scientific Research.
Norway	Norsk Romsenter, Ministry of Trade and Industry.
Poland	Polish Space Office, Ministry of Science and Higher Education.
Portugal	Ministry of Science.
Spain	CDTI, Spanish Centre for the Development of Industrial Technology.
Sweden	Swedish National Space Board, Ministry of Industry, Employment and Communication.
Switzerland	State Secretariat for Education and Research (Swiss Space Office – SSO).
Turkey	TÜBITAK, Scientific and Technical Research Council of Turkey.
United Kingdom	UK Space Agency, Ministry of State Science and Innovation.
United States	NASA, Office of Science and Technology Policy, Executive Office of the President.

1. Most OECD countries do not have a large dedicated space agency, but small teams in ministries or departments, in charge of co-ordinating diverse national space activities. Ministries of defence and other ministries are often involved in selected space programmes. Data are missing for the following OECD countries: Iceland, New Zealand and the Slovak Republic.

the 1980s via bilateral agreements on US and Russian vehicles. Regrouping competences and budgets in one organisation is also a proven means in developing high technologies. The European Space Agency (ESA) is an intergovernmental organisation, which began with a group of countries with maturing national programmes. The co-operation resulted in several successful programmes: a European fleet of launchers, several meteorological and earth observation satellites, major achievements in space sciences, as well as research in advanced telecommunications satellites used profitably by the European industry. Today there are several types of regional groupings tested around the world to provide new entrants with the capabilities of developing their own space systems. Transfers of know-how and interactions with the industry increasingly take place via these established partnerships or less formal regional forums (Box 1.2).

I. THE SPACE SECTOR IN 2011 AND BEYOND

> **Box 1.1. Israel's space programme**
>
> Israel has a vibrant space programme. Administered by the Science Ministry, the Israel Space Agency (ISA) was created in 1983 and led the development of indigenous launchers and satellites. In 1988, the first indigenously built Israeli satellite Ofek 1 was launched using the Shavit rocket, making Israel one of only eight countries that both build their own satellites and launch them. Since then, Israel has launched more than fifteen satellites mainly for security purposes, funded as military programmes. In summer 2010, a new five-year space plan was enacted, with planned ILS 300 million a year investment in the Israeli space programme by 2015 (approximately USD 79.7 million). Industry-wise, aerospace is part of several high-tech activities which play a leading role in Israeli economic growth. It relies on a fairly large defence industry and budget (around 8% of GDP), a wide pool of researchers in the Jewish Diaspora, and engineering and science skills brought by the wave of eastern European and Russian immigrants in the early 1990s (OECD, 2010). Some 25 aerospace and defence-related companies serve Israel's niche market in small high-resolution-imaging satellites, satellite communications systems and derived products. Sales by Israel's space industry represented some USD 800 million in 2009, with key actors including Israel Aerospace Industries (IAI), Elbit, Orbit Alchut Technologies and Rafael.
>
> *Note:* The statistical data for Israel are supplied by and under the responsibility of the relevant Israeli authorities. The use of such data by the OECD is without prejudice to the status of the Golan Heights, East Jerusalem and Israeli settlements in the West Bank under the terms of international law.

> **Box 1.2. Forums for international space co-operation**
>
> The Disaster Monitoring Constellation (DMC): A partnership formed around an international constellation of six satellites, designed and built at Surrey Satellite Technology Ltd. Each satellite is independently owned and controlled by a separate nation, but all satellites have been equally spaced around a sun-synchronous orbit to provide daily imaging capability. It provides independent daily imaging capability to the partner nations, but the imagery is also sold commercially, and distributed freely in times of natural disasters. Countries: Algeria, Nigeria, China, Turkey, the UK and Spain.
>
> Asia-Pacific Regional Space Agency Forum (APRSAF): Forum created in 1993 and revitalised since 2005 to transfer know-how from Japan to other members. Countries: Australia, Bangladesh, Brunei, Bhutan, Canada, Cambodia, China, France, Germany, India, Indonesia, Japan, Korea, Laos, Malaysia, Mongolia, Myanmar, Nepal, New Zealand, Pakistan, Philippines, the Russian Federation, Singapore, Sri Lanka, Thailand, the United States and Viet Nam.
>
> Asia-Pacific Space Cooperation Organization (APSCO): Organisation created in 2005, which became operational in 2008, with a focus on application and training. It builds on the Asia-Pacific Multilateral Cooperation in Space Technology and Applications (AP-MCSTA) convention signed by China, Pakistan and Thailand in 1992. Countries: Bangladesh, China, Indonesia, Iran, Mongolia, Pakistan, Peru, Thailand and Turkey.
>
> Space Conference of the Americas (Conferencia Espacial de las Americas – CEA): Forum started in 1989 to exchange views on Latin American advances in space sciences and applications. Five conferences convened so far (Chile, Uruguay, Colombia, Ecuador, Guatemala and Mexico in late 2010). Countries: Twenty South American countries.

These few examples demonstrate that there are many new entrants in the space community who are actively developing their independent space programmes, with sometimes limited objectives at the start (*e.g.* ground station to receive satellite imagery). In parallel, a number of space-faring countries are clearly widening and in some cases seeking to upgrade their existing capabilities (*e.g.* improved launchers). All this contributes to a changing world map of space powers.

Figure 1.4. **Conservative estimates of space budgets of G20 countries, 2010**
Current USD million

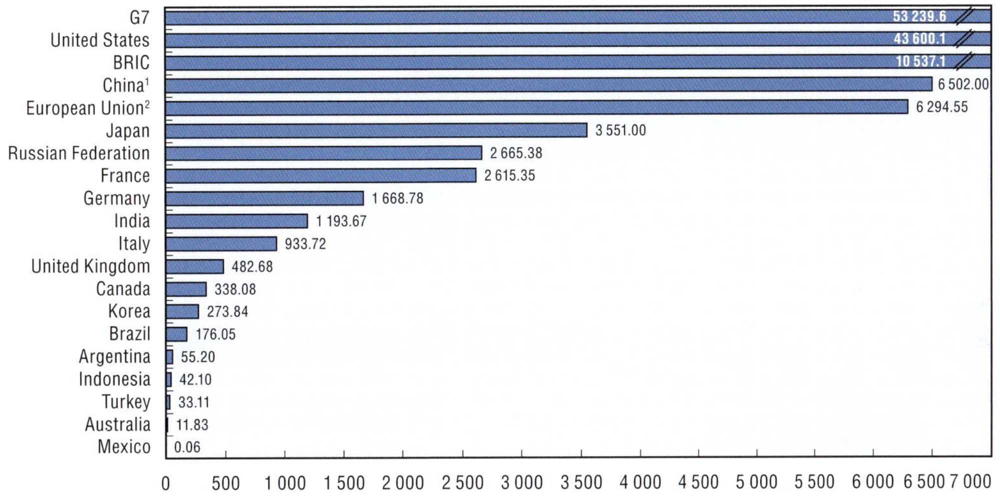

Country	USD million
G7	53 239.6
United States	43 600.1
BRIC	10 537.1
China[1]	6 502.00
European Union[2]	6 294.55
Japan	3 551.00
Russian Federation	2 665.38
France	2 615.35
Germany	1 668.78
India	1 193.67
Italy	933.72
United Kingdom	482.68
Canada	338.08
Korea	273.84
Brazil	176.05
Argentina	55.20
Indonesia	42.10
Turkey	33.11
Australia	11.83
Mexico	0.06

Note: These estimates provide orders of magnitude, as exchange rates may alter direct comparability. Budgets include civil and military budgets. Data missing for Saudi Arabia and South Africa.
1. Unofficial data.
2. For the European Union, only 17 countries with national space budgets are included: Austria, Belgium, Denmark, Finland, France, Germany, Greece, Hungary, Ireland, Italy, Luxembourg, the Netherlands, Norway, Portugal, Spain, Sweden and Switzerland.

StatLink http://dx.doi.org/10.1787/888932400209

The globalisation of the space industry

The new landscape of space-faring nations is also in part the result of the globalisation of the space industry. This globalisation takes place mainly via foreign direct investments and a robust international technology trade, with rising exports and imports of high-technology products and services (OECD, 2009d).

Foreign direct investment (FDI). Foreign direct investment is a particular form of investment, reflecting the establishment of a foreign-affiliated firm under the management of a parent company. FDI often provides a bridge between the host country of a foreign affiliate and the technological resources of foreign multinational corporations (Balasubramanyam *et al.*, 1996). Flows of FDI have expanded rapidly in recent years aided by the removal of many national barriers to capital movements and measures to enhance integration within regional markets (Pain and Wakelin, 1997). These knowledge effects are often called externalities or spillovers, meaning often more to a host country than just building a new plant or subsidiary. As early as the 1990s, commercial satellite manufacturers and operators in OECD countries were seeking potential acquisitions and partners in China, as the nation's accession to the World Trade Organization drew closer. Looking at the comparative advantages of different countries in terms of technological competences, infrastructure and wages, partnering efforts led to the creation of space-related US and European joint-ventures in China, the Russian Federation, India, South Africa and other countries.

All large OECD space manufacturers now have joint ventures in non-OECD countries despite sometimes complex rules. In the Russian Federation for example, a 2008 federal law imposes prior governmental approval for foreign acquisitions which would result in 50% and more foreign ownership in a company operating in one of 42 designated strategic sectors. The sectors include: defence-related activities, high-technology and dual-purpose sectors in particular space-related technologies and aviation (OECD, 2009c). On a global scale, aerospace foreign direct investments already represent large investments and important knowledge transfers. In a recent report by AeroStrategy (2009), investments in joint ventures accounted for some 59% of the value chain investments done by 121 major aerospace manufacturers over the past 20 years, representing some USD 531 billion (Figure 1.5). Although this concerns mainly the aeronautic field (*e.g.* building aircraft components in a foreign country), satellite manufacturing follows the same trend.

Figure 1.5. **Aerospace globalisation speeding up via large investments in joint ventures**

Major chain investments by 121 Aerospace Original Equipment Manufacturers (1990-2009)
Percentage and USD billion

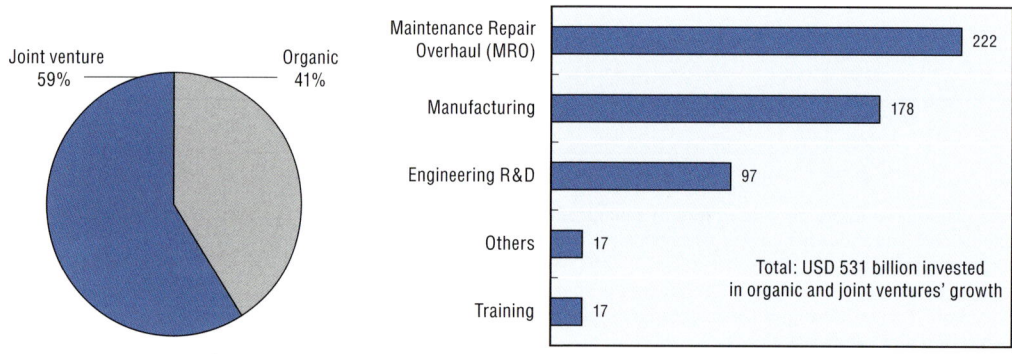

Source: AeroStrategy (2009).

In general, manufacturing plants are often originally established to serve as outlets for sales and distribution or for low-value added manufacturing (*e.g.* components), rather than centres for research and high-value added manufacturing. This is changing however. In BRIC countries, large- and medium-size enterprises have shifted from imitation to innovation, and greatly facilitated the absorption and adaptation of advanced foreign technologies. Transfers of space technologies have had a positive effect on satellite technological efforts in many developing countries, as one can see from the development of indigenous satellite programmes in many parts of the world.

Foreign direct investments are also increasingly international in nature, as the new international players China and India are now themselves investing in OECD countries. To close the technology gap with well established aerospace players, suppliers in China and India have set up partnering arrangements or have made acquisitions to become more firmly entrenched in the global supply chain. There are already many examples in the aeronautic sector. As an illustration of this globalisation, as future aircraft will increasingly make use of composites, the Xian Aircraft division of China Aviation Industry (AVIC) bought in fall 2009 some 91.25% of Austria's Fischer Advanced Composite Components (FACC), a company supplying customers including Airbus, Alenia Aeronautica, Boeing, Bombardier, Embraer, Eurocopter and Gulfstream.

Trade in space technologies. Foreign direct investments represent only one aspect of space industry globalisation. The other one concerns the trade of technologies. In most countries, space technologies are considered strategic in nature due to their dual use capacities (*i.e.* used for both military and civilian purposes). The trade of sensitive technologies is therefore ruled by strict export control policies, which have been strengthened over the years in some countries, making it harder for industry to transfer satellite technologies and know-how. In the United States, changes to the International Traffic in Arms Regulations (ITAR) regime in the 1990s have had the effect of slowing down exports of the US space industry and boosting competitors from other countries, who build ITAR-free satellites, *i.e.* with no American components. Although international trade of space technologies has increased over the years as more actors have entered the scene, a key component in technology transfers concerns the multiplication of industrial offset agreements, which compel the exporters to transfer specific know-how and materials to local industry players. Following the Russian Federation's example in the 1990s, China and India have become new sources for international space technology trade for emerging economies, as demonstrated by increased technical co-operation with South American countries, such as Bolivia, Brazil, Peru and Venezuela. China and India were seen in the late 1990s as emerging space powers, despite having started their respective space programmes decades earlier. Today both countries are full-blown space powers, each with ever-growing capabilities, which parallel their rising economic importance on the world's stage (see spotlight sections on India and China in this publication).

2. The space economy as an engine of economic growth

The space sector plays an increasingly pivotal role in the efficient functioning of modern societies and their economic development. Despite its usual reliance on relatively high institutional investments up-front, space can increasingly be seen as a source of economic growth. This is demonstrated by the growing importance of the space economy, the way the sector fared during the economic crisis and new commercial activities on the horizon.

The growing importance of the space economy

The use of satellite technology in navigation, communications, meteorology, and earth observation is giving rise to a growing stream of applications in such areas as transport, natural resources management, agriculture, environmental and climate change monitoring, entertainment and so on, which are in turn creating new downstream uses and new markets. The space economy therefore includes new products and services using space systems' unique capacities, such as data links (*e.g.* satellite communications' relays) or data garnered in space (*e.g.* satellite imagery, positioning data). Larger than the traditional space sector (*e.g.* rockets and satellites), the space economy involves geographic information systems developers and navigation equipment sellers.

Mapping the space economy is a complex process, although there are indications that products and services are growing rapidly. Estimates vary widely, and many involve some degree of double counting. But the most reliable estimates suggest that the revenues derived from space products and services amounted to some USD 150-165 billion in 2009, including space manufacturing's direct revenues and space-related services (*e.g.* leases of transponders on satellites). The estimates for the main commercial markets for space services, which are detailed in later sections, include:

- Telecommunications (lease of transponders and communications via satellite): USD 11-to-15 billion.

I. THE SPACE SECTOR IN 2011 AND BEYOND

- Satellite broadcasting (television via satellite): USD 65-to-72 billion.
- Earth observation products and services: USD 850 million to USD 1 billion market.
- In addition, the geospatial and geopositioning markets build at least in part on satellite capacities (*e.g.* GPS signals). The navigation and positioning industry represented USD 15 billion in revenue in 2009 (around 75% captured by four main actors: Trimble Navigation Limited, MiTAC International Corporation, TomTom and Garmin).

To put these numbers in perspective, Figure 1.6 provides some rough estimates of the revenues generated by institutional investments in space developments over a decade (1996-2005). The estimated USD 175-200 billion invested in space programmes worldwide has contributed to some USD 440-645 billion in revenues for the entire value chain of the space sector. Space services, which include in particular the profitable telecommunications and broadcasting services (*i.e.* satellite television), provide the larger share of revenues, up to USD 325 billion over the period. In addition, indirect industrial effects amounting to USD 350-600 billion and diverse social effects are contributing additional benefits to the initial investments. These impacts are examined in more detail in Chapter IV.

Figure 1.6. **Estimates on the generation of direct and indirect economic benefits, derived from space activities (1996-2005 period)**

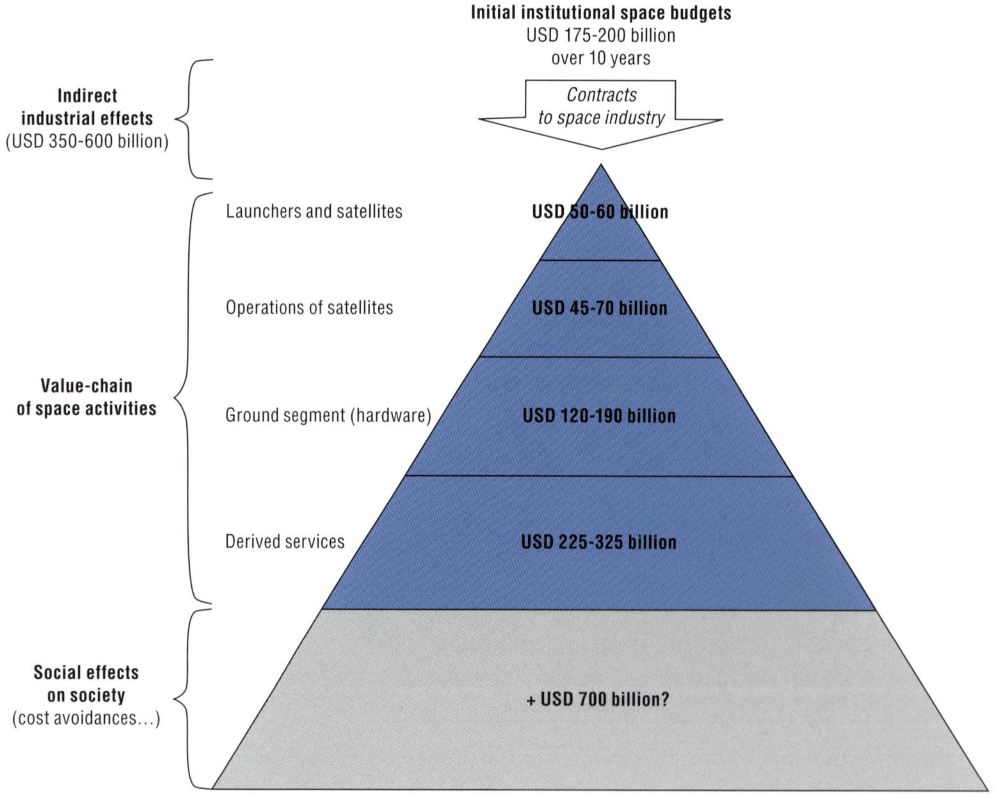

Initial institutional space budgets
USD 175-200 billion
over 10 years

Contracts to space industry

Indirect industrial effects (USD 350-600 billion)

Value-chain of space activities:
- Launchers and satellites: USD 50-60 billion
- Operations of satellites: USD 45-70 billion
- Ground segment (hardware): USD 120-190 billion
- Derived services: USD 225-325 billion

Social effects on society (cost avoidances…): + USD 700 billion?

Source: Adapted from Cohendet (2010).

Faring well during the economic crisis

Despite the economic crisis, the space sector has fared relatively well since 2008; several factors have contributed to this good economic health. Space remains a strategic sector, often sheltered because of national imperatives and institutional funding. In addition many countries are now investing in space technologies to advance national objectives. The cyclical nature of the industry (*i.e.* the need to replenish the fleet of satellites regularly) as well as the continuing commercial success of many space services has contributed to the dynamism of the entire value chain.

Telecommunications still represent in early 2011 the main commercial space market, and several satellite operators have broken records in revenues since the beginning of the economic crisis. The industry's inherent long lead time to procure, build and launch satellites somewhat shelters the sector, as current activities are a reflection of projects already planned a number of years ago. However, their general economic base has been relatively unaffected by the crisis (*i.e.* people still want to watch television, military customers still want to communicate and ships at sea still want to send data). In that context, the satellite telecommunications operators have positioned themselves well, benefitting from growing mass markets (*e.g.* satellite television broadcasting) and a robust demand from institutional users (*i.e.* defence, new customers in the developing world, development of anchor contracts to cover the needs of different administrations). Future growth in broadband via satellite and more traditional telecommunications Fixed-Satellite Services (FSS) are also confirmed by ITU data on satellite network co-ordination request submissions. Those submissions made in the last two years give an indication of the satellite networks planned to be brought into use over the 2012-15 period, and they show strong applications in all three main bands (C, Ku and Ka) by existing operators. Another ITU indicator of the dynamism of the satellite industry is the updating of the list of operating administrations/agencies in operational control of the ground stations (*i.e.* mandatory information to be provided with the satellite network filing submissions). More than 20 new operating agencies have been submitted to the ITU Radiocommunication Bureau since 2008, underlining the growth in the industry (International Telecommunications Union, 2009).

This positive situation in telecommunications has impacted the rest of the value chain in the space sector: the main satellite manufacturers have also experienced a stable market for commercial telecom geostationary satellites. They received 30 contracts in 2009 and 26 contracts in 2010, with an expected trend of a minimum of 20 contracts until 2015. The institutional demand for satellites remains relatively strong and geographically diversified, particularly for military/dual-use satellites, and small earth observation satellites. The total five-year value of satellite production is estimated at some USD 65.5 billion (Forecast International, 2011, see Figure 1.7).

In this rather favourable context, the sector has overall not suffered much from financing difficulties, despite the specificities of the satellite industry. In the case of the satellite telecommunications sector, the high profitability of satellite services over the past 15 years has allowed operators to benefit from classic financial schemes (*e.g.* equity financing, bond issuance) to develop their activities. Several operators have become publicly traded corporations. They have also resorted to project financing, with syndicates of banks providing loans. This successful trend in financing satellite telecommunications has led to similar, if limited, experiences in other domains of space activities. For example, DigitalGlobe, a satellite imaging company, launched initial public offerings of stocks in 2009 and 2010, using the proceeds to build its next generation of satellites.

Figure 1.7. **Five-year value of satellite production estimated at USD 65.5 billion**
Estimates in USD billion and percentage

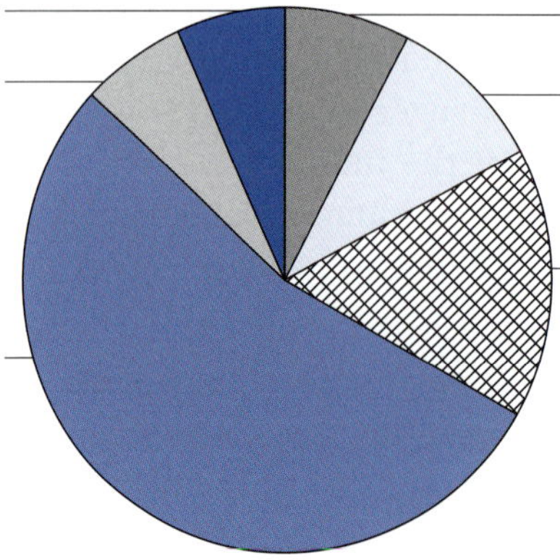

- Space Systems/Loral (US), USD 3.8 billion, 6.7%
- Boeing (US), USD 3.6 billion, 6.4%
- All others, USD 30.4 billion, 53.7%
- Thales Alenia Space (Europe), USD 4.3 billion, 7.6%
- EADS Astrium (Europe), USD 5.4 billion, 9.5%
- Lockheed Martin (US), USD 9.1 billion, 16.1%

Source: Forecast International (2011).

But a relatively recent trend is for satellite operators to receive loan guarantees from national export credit agencies to fund their satellite fleets. In the aeronautic sector, airlines have received export-credit agency backing for years to buy aircraft, in addition to using conventional debt and equity markets, and a multinational agreement among developed nations fixes limits on export credit financing systems (OECD, 2008c). The French Coface has been particularly active since the beginning of the economic crisis, supporting the projects of customers of European space manufacturers with more than USD 3.5 billion as of late 2010. For example, the American Iridium mobile operator received in 2010 a record loan guarantee totalling 95% of USD 1.8 billion, for its contract with the European satellite manufacturer Thales Alenia Space, for the construction of 72 operational satellites plus spares. The support of national export credit agencies is widespread internationally. Export Development Canada provided credit financing to Ukraine in late 2009 to buy a satellite from the Canadian MacDonald, Dettwiler and Associates. And in late 2010, China Development Bank provided a commercial loan to Bolivia for its first communication satellite, for 85% of its estimated USD 300 million value, procured by to Chinese companies.

This overall positive environment for the space sector, in the midst of a serious economic crisis, may not last indefinitely. On the commercial front, despite the growth of space applications and the financial success of satellite telecommunications, the main operators will reach the end of a cycle over the next three years, having placed all the contracts for replenishing their respective fleets of satellites. But more importantly, the space sector manufacturers are still dependent on institutional budgets for much of the research and development in satellites and launchers. Key customers for small and large satellites are also still governments. The potential restrictions in budgets in many countries, in science and defence particularly, may affect the industry over the next three years, as budget cuts filter down the entire value chain. Some possible impacts of the economic crisis are summarised in Box 1.3.

The possible downturn in commercial and institutional space activities will probably not be general. As shown earlier, new entrants in the space sector are based in every continent, including countries with strong economic prospects, who are all investing in indigenous programmes and importing technologies and know-how (e.g. Brazil, China and India). And as of early 2011, budgets for space activities remain stable and are even on the rise for a number of OECD countries (e.g. France, Germany and the United States).

> **Box 1.3. Possible impacts of the economic crisis on the space sector**
>
> The current and planned reductions in public R&D funding and science budgets in many OECD and non-OECD countries could have at least some limited impacts in space agencies and space industry contracts over the next five years:
>
> - Less institutional demand for services in some countries (*i.e.* expected defence cuts).
> - Actions of possible protectionism (*i.e.* proactively protecting captive markets).
> - Less financing on international markets (*e.g.* difficulty in funding upcoming projects; high risk ventures not supported).
> - Harsher competitive environment for commercial stakeholders, with rise of new actors.
> - Despite strong demand, intense cost pressures on satellite suppliers to build more cheaply.
> - More players than the communications' markets can sustain (MSS and FSS operators markets).
> - Overcapacity in the launch sector not translating into lower prices for satellite operators (Sea launch should again join the small club of launch companies) due to growing Asian competition over the next decade.

Commercial space growing and governments adapting

Most of the satellites launched today are developed to serve institutional missions (*e.g.* defence, meteorology, climate and science). The role of public institutions remains essential in the space sector, not only in terms of the necessary investments in R&D, but also as anchor customers for many space products and services. However the trend to commercialisation of space activities is still strong, as shown by two indicators: the increasing number of commercial actors in the sector, and the rapid development of national space laws, simplifying the rules of the road for institutional and commercial actors alike.

Since the late 1980s, the number of commercial actors involved in space activity has increased. Industry is active not only in traditional space powers, but also in countries with more recent space programmes. There is for example a growing geographical diversity of satellite manufacturers bidding for commercial satellite contracts, as shown in Figure 1.8.

The number of smaller firms at different levels of the space sector's value chain is also increasing, improving the prospects for economic growth, as small and medium companies play a major role in driving innovation, especially in knowledge-based industries (OECD, 2003). However the competition is getting fiercer at lower tiers. For example, as the space industries of smaller European countries have been growing (*e.g.* 30 firms in Finland, 20 firms in Denmark), more small firms than ever before are competing for places in larger consortia, to bid for European Space Agency contracts.

In addition to these trends, the growth in space-related entrepreneurial activity in the space industry has been ongoing, particularly in the United States. Despite the economic crisis, there are many companies pursuing the development of new commercial space operations, vying to transport cargo and passengers in suborbital and/or orbital flights (*e.g.* Virgin Galactic, SpaceX, Bigelow, Orbital Sciences, Xcor and Armadillo Aerospace). The total investment committed to the commercial spaceflight industry is estimated at USD 1.46 billion in 2009, with over USD 300 million in new commitments since January of 2008 (Tauri Group, 2010). A significant aspect is the source of funding for this fledging industry, dubbed sometimes the "new space" industry, which is mainly based on "angel' investors" (Figure 1.9).

Figure 1.8. **Satellite orders per main satellite manufacturer in March 2010**

Number of orders and percentage (total orders: 46 satellites)

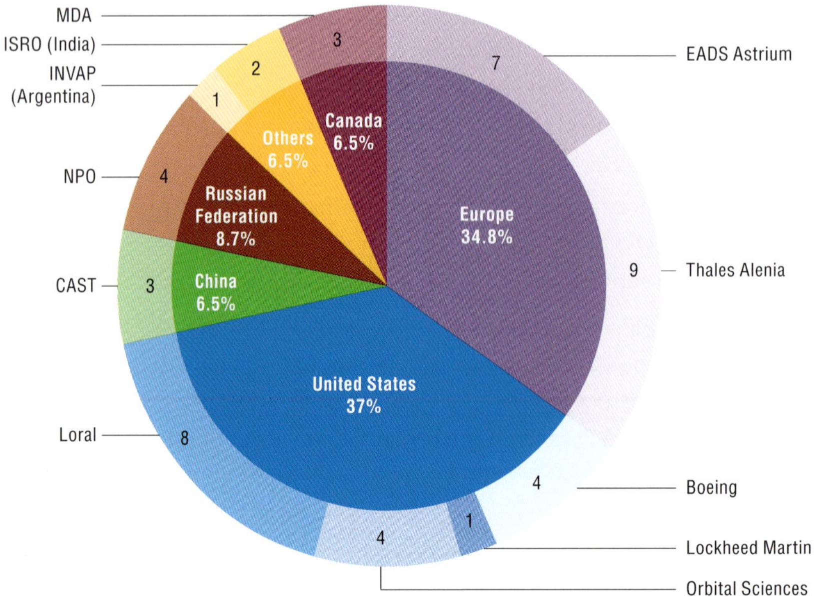

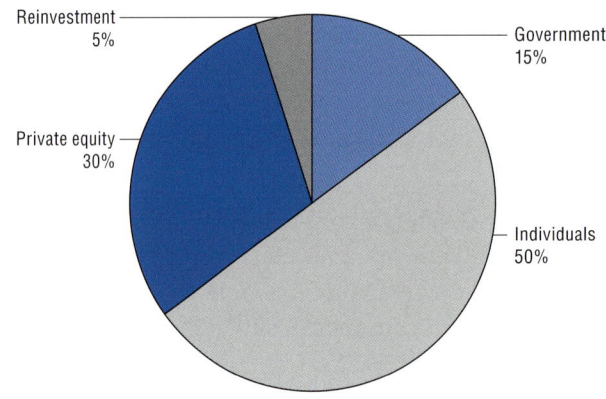

Source: Lardier (2010).

Figure 1.9. **Investment in commercial spaceflight by source, 2009**

Source: Tauri Group (2010).

All these developments demonstrate that space programmes increasingly involve commercial actors, as providers of systems but also as investors. In this context, there is a strong move in many space-faring countries to move from a mainly treaty-based international legal and regulatory regime for space activities, to more commercially-oriented national regimes.

During the 1960s and 1970s, a number of basic treaties and principles have been enacted internationally concerning the peaceful uses and non-appropriation of outer space. Based on this regime, governments are liable under international space law whenever a space object is launched from their territory, even if it is by a private entity. To mitigate the risks, and provide a business-friendly framework, governments can develop an appropriate national licensing structure that regulates institutional and private space activities taking place on their soil.

Since the 1980s, the rapid progression of commercial space activities that followed the privatisation of international telecommunications organisations, such as Intelsat and Eutelsat, has spurred the swift development of national laws and regulations worldwide. With the development of the commercial space industry, it became possible for a country to rather easily "buy" satellite imagery, an entire satellite or a launch opportunity for its own spacecraft. Over the years, several space-faring countries have therefore passed legislation establishing more clearly how their national governments interpret international law, and making the rules of the game more transparent to private firms (Figure 1.10).

Figure 1.10. **Development of space laws: The rise of national laws and regulations (1957-2010)**

Number of treaties, national space laws and regulations per year[1]

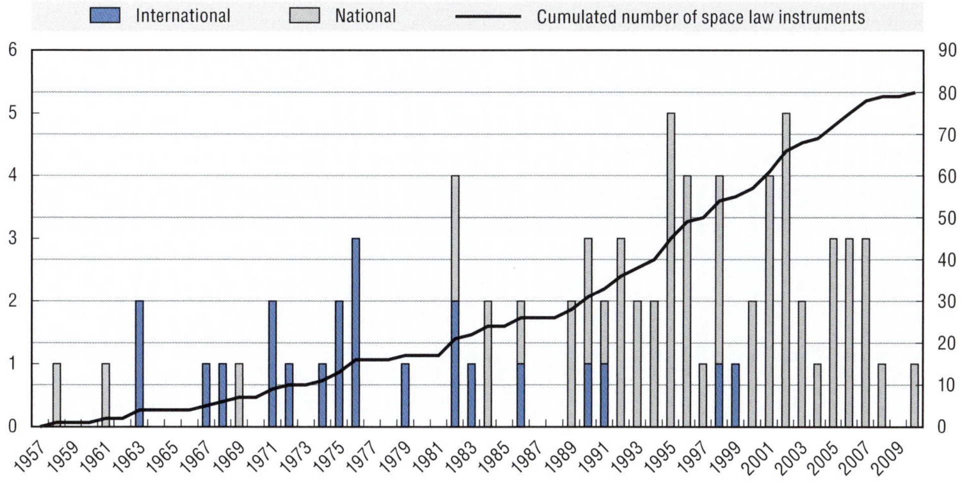

1. International instruments include the United Nations space-related treaties and principles, international conventions creating multilateral organisations (ESA, Intelsat...) and other international agreements. National space laws and regulations include several instruments (in some cases major updates to existing regulations), as referenced by the United Nations Office of Outer Space Affairs.

Source: OECD calculations, based on the United Nations data (2010).

A diversity of governments are developing space laws, not only long-established space-faring nations (e.g. the United States, France, the Russian Federation, Japan), but also countries with limited space activities wishing to either attract new investments from abroad, or to cater to the needs of their own fledging space industry (e.g. supporting development of small satellite missions). In the case of satellite remote sensing, the current trend for many countries is not to have an overall national set of rules but to set up specific policies on a satellite-by-satellite basis (who is requesting data and why). When there is no national law, users and distributors fill the void and seek guidance on a daily basis with domestic regulations. Often, the only legal bases for data distribution lie in the contracts between the national data receiving entity and the foreign satellite data provider. The enactment of a national legal and regulatory regime for space activities can be an important component when trying to develop a competitive space industry (Box 1.4). Having a clear institutional framework for space activities plays a key role for sustainable and cost-effective space systems, as confirmed by the recommendations that came out of a 2004 OECD project on space commercialisation.

> **Box 1.4. Competitiveness in space**
>
> The "competitiveness in space" of a given country depends on the country's starting conditions. These "framework" conditions encompass the institutional and structural features that characterise a country in comparison with others in terms of development (OECD, 2005). Competitiveness depends therefore on a number of factors. Concerning space activities in general, once the basic infrastructures are in place (*e.g.* laboratories, R&D centers, even limited manufacturing) with relatively stable institutions, only innovation, such as new technologies and applications, can keep the momentum going. Competitiveness, then, is not about absolutes but about being able to make the most of the foundations that a country has already developed. This includes the regulatory framework to facilitate private capital to foster commercial telecommunications activities for example. At an early stage in a space programme, real strides can be made by the rapid take up of advanced technologies (*e.g.* going from no communications infrastructure at all in some places to satellite downlinks, thus bypassing the need to install expensive ground infrastructure). However in the long run, stable foundations for space activities remain a key asset for competitiveness (*e.g.* sustainable budgets for R&D and operations, human resources). All the factors are interdependent, as none of these alone can ensure competitiveness and cost-effectiveness. For example, the value of increased spending on long-term R&D will be undermined if rigidities in the labor market and other institutional weaknesses make it difficult for new graduates to gain access to suitable employment opportunities in the space sector.

3. Preserving a skilled workforce in the space sector

Numerous reports have been written over the past decade highlighting apparent shortages of particular skills in certain fields in the aerospace sector, or offering forecasts of expected skill gaps among the working population in OECD countries. A number of issues influence directly and indirectly the current state and the future of the workforce in the space sector. But the potential scarcity of talent might in some cases be overstated, as external factors such as the international mobility of talents are underestimated.

The demographic factor

The baby boom generation is reaching retirement age in most industrialised countries. In addition, despite moderate growth in a few countries since the mid-1990s (*e.g.* France, the United Kingdom, Sweden), fertility rates across the OECD are typically below replacement, with overall an ageing population, with the notable exceptions of Mexico and Turkey (OECD, 2009f). This large wave of retirement is affecting all sectors of the economy, including the space sector.

Many of the engineers and scientists who have worked on space systems in OECD countries over the past three decades are retiring; however countries have different problems in terms of their space-related workforce (ESF, 2003). There is generally a sharp decrease in the engineering and scientific population under 30 years old in most OECD countries, but the main difficulty faced by a number of actors, space agencies and industry alike, could come from the "missing generation", *i.e.* a gap in the overall workforce. There might not be enough experienced future managers to take over large programmes.

- In France, the demographic trends should translate into the departure by 2015 of 45% to 50% of the entire aerospace workforce active in 1999 (Lejeune and Nosmas, 2004). The decade-long French policy of recruiting young employees, while having fifty-five year olds retire early, has created a generational gap in some sectors, with a loss of expertise and lack of enough mid-level management to supervise new younger workers coming into the sector.

- In Germany, the economy could have a shortfall of 220 000 engineers by 2014, according to a study by the Cologne Institute for Economic Research, including major gaps in the aerospace industry. Already, about 2 000 high-technology engineering vacancies could not be filled in 2010.

- In the United States, NASA's workforce under 30 years of age is estimated to be one-third the size of its workforce over 60. Already by 2011, some 28% of NASA's engineers and 45% of its scientists could be eligible to retire (National Research Council, 2007). The American Aerospace Industries Association developed a parametric model to try and forecast the supply and demand of aerospace and defence industry professionals and helps quantify the deficit of scientists and engineers, as reported by Maloney *et al.* (2007). It computed the annual number of graduates with science and engineering degrees, separating out non-US citizens and those who choose not to work in the defence industry. Assuming that public spending would remain relatively stable, the model showed a deficit of aerospace/defence industry scientists and engineers for each year beginning in 2005, extending through 2020. As an illustration, the year 2012 should see the greatest deficit with a shortage of more than 34 000 scientists and engineers, compensated in later years as the wave of retirements slowly diminishes (Aerospace Industries Association, 2008).

- In contrast, the age distribution in more recent space powers, such as China and India, shows the emergence of a new generation of young scientists and engineers, supervised by managers who are just a generation above them. For example, 60% of the Chinese Center for Earth Observation and Digital Earth's workforce is 35 years old or less (Center for Earth Observation and Digital Earth, 2010).

Attracting and retaining workers in space programmes

Despite the fact that over the past 15 years, most OECD and non-OECD economies have experienced a large increase in the number of students in higher education, attracting the best engineers and scientists to work in the space sector is not as easy as it used to be (Willis, 2009). This trend is linked in part to a general disaffection towards science and technology-related careers by students in many countries, the perceived volatility of the sector, a possible mismatch between training and actual employment opportunities in many countries.

Mathematics and sciences are still needed in the space sector. The majority of jobs available in the space sector can be found in the scientific and engineering fields. In the aerospace sector as a whole, there has been much progress in terms of automating certain research processes, thanks to a growing proficiency with powerful PC workstations and the use of Math Libraries or commercially available software packages. The development of computational fluid dynamics for example has benefitted significantly from progress in computer simulation. However, many observers in the profession stress the need for future engineers to still understand the underlying physics to be able to judiciously choose a numerical procedure to achieve the best simulations (Shang, 2004). This required judgment can only be nurtured through thorough education and training.

Taking stock of the diminishing attractiveness of scientific studies in OECD countries. Over the years, the OECD has studied the interest in science and technology studies among young people via different mechanisms. The OECD Programme for International Student Assessment (PISA) assesses and compares the performance of 15-year-olds in reading, mathematics and science competencies (OECD, 2007). The PISA database includes information on nearly 400 000 students from 57 countries (OECD, 2009e). When asked to choose a field of research which 15-year-old students would pursue as a scientist, most students chose the treatment and cure of diseases, or space science. The first one is much more popular with girls than boys but the difference is much narrower in the case of space. The two most common reasons for the choice of field of research involve references to curiosity, interest, excitement and to helping people. This finding tends to demonstrate that space is *a priori* a very attractive field for young students, should they decide to pursue a scientific or engineering programme in later years. The challenge is to have some of them choose that general path.

A European Science Foundation study mentions the following reasons for the student's lack of interest in scientific studies and careers (based on an opinion poll aimed at European young people still studying in 2001 in EU member states): lack of appeal of scientific studies (67.3% of respondents); difficulty of the subjects (58.7%); young people are not so interested in scientific subjects (53.4%); salaries are not attractive enough (40%); science has too negative an image (34%) (ESF, 2003). In 2006 the OECD Global Science Forum led an OECD-wide analysis to determine whether the perceived decline in science and technology could actually be measured (OECD, 2008b). The absolute number of students in science and technology fields shows an overall increase, but aggregate numbers hide important differences among disciplines. Engineering students account for 40% to 60% of science and technology students in most OECD countries, especially at the new entrant and graduate levels, with a stable or increased enrolment trend over the past 10 years. The situation for physical sciences and mathematics is the opposite, with the proportion of students in some countries halved between 1995 and 2003. The proportion of students in the life sciences has remained mostly stable, due primarily to an increasing number of female students, while the number of computer science students has increased dramatically. This particular evolution may be the consequence of shifts in student choice within the overall domain of science and technology (*i.e.* from pure physics to computer studies), but also in the perception they get from potential sectors of employment and the space sector is not immune to this trend.

A *perceived volatile sector*. The students' decisions about study and career paths are primarily based upon interest in a particular field, and on their perception of job prospects in that field. Accurate knowledge about science and technology professions and career prospects are key elements of orientation, but are currently fraught with stereotypes and incomplete information. In that context, the aerospace sector is often perceived as a complex and volatile sector by the general public. Since the early 1990s, many restructuration efforts have taken place in the aerospace and defence industries in Europe, Japan, the Russian Federation and North America to make the companies more productive and less prone to the cyclical nature of the aeronautic, space and military markets. This situation has affected the number of people employed in those sectors. From dozens of firms, several large companies have been created, thus reducing the number of jobs available. The space sector has been particularly affected, with often reduced institutional budgets and the "freezing" of the number of jobs offered in both space agencies and industry.

Since the mid-2000s, the situation has evolved, boosted by renewed institutional space budgets in some countries and a large demand for space services. Many large space manufacturers and subcontractors (*e.g.* propulsion, electronics) have become more competitive internationally, while several space applications sectors have been developing and hiring (*e.g.* telecommunications and satellite earth observation operators).

Paradoxically enough, the industrial restructuring efforts of the 1990s are being reversed somehow in the 2010s by the appearance and expansion of new actors in the space industry increasing competition in the sector (*e.g.* emergent start-ups in commercial space transportation in the United States) or reinforcing national space capabilities (*e.g.* OHB and Rapid Eye in Germany). In the short term, this may offer more job prospects in some regions or countries, but to the detriment of other industries/areas of employment.

Mismatch between training and actual employment opportunities. Although there are numerous calls to increase the number of engineers and scientists over the next years in OECD countries, there is paradoxically in some cases a relative scarcity of "space jobs" available to young graduates and mid-career professionals. This comes from a mismatch between training and actual employment opportunities.

Looking at specific scientific fields, several examples are quite telling. The total number of astronomers for instance has grown worldwide, almost exponentially between 1960 and 2000. The membership of the International Astronomical Union, for instance, increased from about 1 200 in 1961 to 9 000 in 2003 (Metcalfe, 2008). In the case of the United States, Seth *et al.* (2009) estimate in their position paper for the *US Decadal Survey for Astronomy*, that there are not enough permanent positions in the field for all astronomy PhDs, taking into account existing limited employment demographics. The number of astronomy and astrophysics PhDs awarded in the US from 1999-2005 has been roughly constant, with around 170 PhDs awarded per year. These numbers represent a 70% increase over the number of astronomy and astrophysics PhDs awarded in 1985, as since then the total inflation-adjusted astronomy budget has doubled. However, based on available job offers, the graduates are currently vying for only 60-90 estimated positions annually, suggesting that only 35% to 55% of astronomy PhDs receive permanent jobs in astronomy (Williams *et al.*, 2009). One foreseen approach to counter this problem would be to inform would-be astronomers of the scarcity of existing jobs, and create possible channels to work in other related disciplines.

Space activities offer a large diversity of jobs, with competences that may often be also applicable in aeronautics, defence, and information technologies, to name just a few. Changing specialities in high technology sectors can sometimes be difficult, although young to mid-career scientists and engineers are often the most adaptable. Some large space and defence firms have put in place new recruiting policies, requiring employees to be more mobile and able to work on different dual systems when needed (*e.g.* moving from civil space projects to military ones). This versatility can be used to improve competitiveness and relocate manpower, whenever programmes can use similar if not exactly the same competences. This can be already a well-defined corporate practice, as for example a given engineer may know from the start that he/she could work on different activities throughout his/her career (*e.g.* Dassault). In a number of large aerospace and defence groups, increased linkages between organic divisions are sought, as in the case in early 2009 between EADS defence and Astrium space divisions (Guillermard, 2009).

Overall, despite the perceived volatility and the inherent cyclical nature of the sector, there seem to be more employment opportunities in 2011 than a decade earlier in the space sector, in both OECD and non-OECD countries. This trend could intensify as demography helps generations of scientists and engineers move up the hierarchical ladder of their organisations, opening up more junior positions to young graduates. The main challenge for the space sector will be to compete with other sectors for the scientifically minded students, as many future scientists and engineers look at other sectors for technical challenges or better salaries (*e.g.* software development, biotechnologies).

Towards more international mobility of the space workforce

There is a rapidly growing demand for highly skilled workers, which is leading to a global competition for talent (OECD, 2008d). Many OECD countries and a growing range of non-member economies aim to attract the same set of highly skilled researchers and scientists. The mobility of human resources in science and technology (HRST) has become a central aspect of globalisation, and the same is true for many professionals in the space sector, despite specific hurdles (*e.g.* some jobs are reserved for nationals). Migration of HRST now plays an important role in shaping skilled labour forces across the world, and most OECD countries are already net beneficiaries of highly skilled migration, with current inflows of skilled people larger than outflows (OECD, 2008a). This trend is also impacting employment in strategic sectors, such as the space sector.

Talents from emerging space countries. Starting in the late 1970s and 1980s, a number of newly industrialised countries have developed their own aerospace and defence industries (*e.g.* Argentina, Brazil, India, Indonesia, Israel, South Korea and South Africa). They are now participating in the internationalisation of the aerospace supply chains, especially as major Western aerospace and defence groups have moved away from manufacturing some of their products to become systems integrators, assembling together the products of foreign contractors (Goldstein, 2002). In addition, some countries – particularly India and China – have adopted strong voluntary policies to develop curricula focused on science and technology, resulting in large pools of talent (Goldman, 2008). To illustrate those trends, data are provided below. Comparisons must be exercised with care, as the data were often developed using different methodologies and definitions.

With an estimated 1.4 million researchers, China now ranks second behind the United States and is also the world's second highest investor in R&D after the United States (Gallagher, 2009). In addition to aerospace, priority is currently given to energy and water resources, environmental protection, information technology, biotechnology and advanced materials. Between 1995 and 2000, the number of doctorates in science and engineering conferred by Chinese universities increased 140%, from 518 to 1 247, surpassing India in 1997 (Saxenian and Quan, 2005). To further improve its programmes, China has largely invested in its universities, also hiring foreign-trained faculty (French, 2005). In 2002, China graduated some 219 000 engineers (in that particular study, the US comparable figure was less than 60 000), representing some 39% of all Chinese college graduates. When physical sciences are included, this figure climbs to 60% of all degrees awarded (compared with 17% for the United States) (Gross and Heinold, 2005). But those figures coming from different studies do not take into account wide variation in the quality of education at the regional and even sub-regional, level. As noted in the recent OECD reviews of Chinese tertiary education, the very rapid expansion of the past decade in terms of university development (student enrolments in tertiary education have expanded from 5-to-25 million in some 15 years) is now slowing down, in an effort to address concerns about quality, equity and apparent imbalances between graduate supply and labour market demand (Gallagher, 2009). India's intake in approved engineering colleges was estimated at some 360 000 in 2002-03, with the number of college enrolees in science and engineering representing more than 30% (Gross and Heinold, 2005). In 2004, China and India together awarded some 463 000 bachelor's degrees in engineering, computer science, and information technology, more than triple the number of American graduates (Gereffi and Wadhwa, 2005).

Despite the fact that China and India award more degrees in engineering, computer science and information technology in absolute numbers compared with the United States, data normalised against country population reveal that the United States still produces a good number of engineers (Figure 1.11). China has roughly four times the population of the United States and India is approximately three times as large. The data normalised against country population show that per every one million citizens, the United States produces roughly 750 technology specialists, compared with 500 in China and 200 in India.

Figure 1.11. **Engineering degrees awarded in the United States, China and India, 2004**
Total number of degrees awarded and number of degrees awarded per million citizens

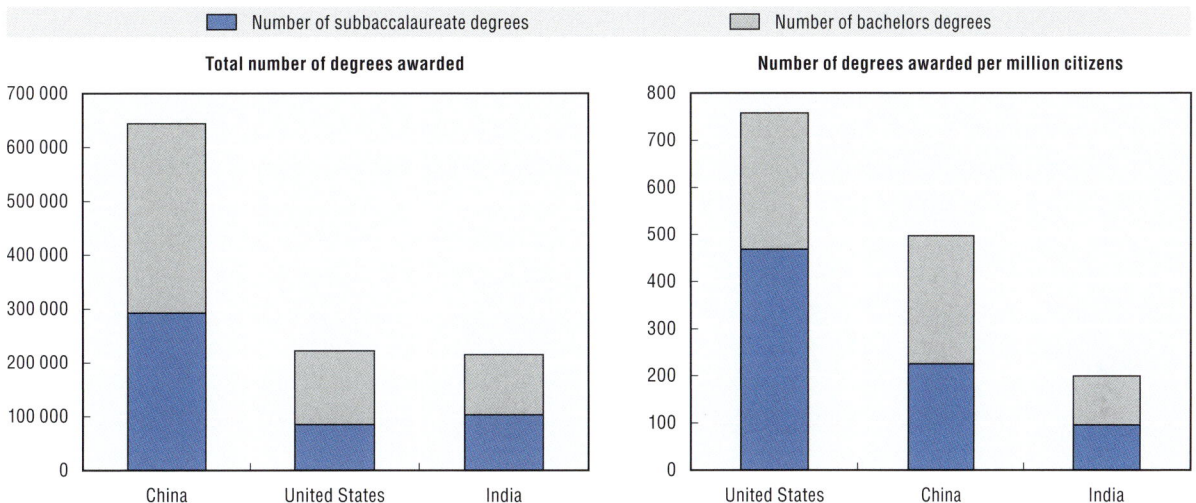

Note: Subbaccalaureate degrees refer to Associates degrees in the United States, short-cycle degrees in China and three-year diplomas in India. Degrees include: engineering, computer science and information technology degrees.
Source: Adapted from Gereffi and Wadhwa (2005).

However the rise in the number of new engineers in selected space-faring countries needs to be analysed qualitatively and not just quantitatively. For example, according to some analysis, fewer than 10% of Chinese graduates would be suitable to work in international high-end service occupations because of theoretical, rather than practical knowledge (Farrell and J. Grant, 2005). But it remains that the pool of talent is growing, as the number of researchers increases worldwide (Figure 1.12).

Figure 1.12. **Number of researchers and average annual growth**
Full-time equivalents (number of researchers in 2007 or most recent year in parentheses)

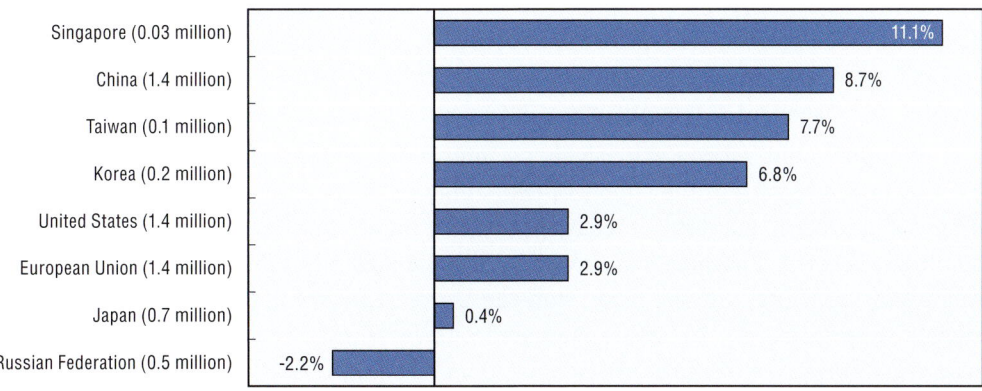

Source: OECD (2009b) and National Science Foundation (2010).
StatLink http://dx.doi.org/10.1787/888932400228

More foreign born PhDs in OECD countries. Virtually all OECD countries aim to attract highly-skilled immigrants for their university, research and high-technology sectors, and this also impacts the space sector (OECD, 2009a). The report *The Global Competition for Talent: Mobility of the Highly Skilled* (OECD, 2008d) established an inventory of government policy practices and programmes to encourage the inward and outward international mobility of human resources in science and technology (HRST), including doctorate holders, doctoral students and researchers. Policies range from economic incentives to encourage inflows, immigration-oriented assistance, recognition procedures for foreign qualifications, social and cultural support, and support for research abroad. One general finding is that as the OECD foreign-born populations grow rapidly, the pool of talent also increases.

Canada. According to Statistics Canada, Asia, and in particular China and India, have become the major source of foreign born PhDs in Canada since the beginning of the 1980s, whereas the United States and the United Kingdom, the two dominant sources prior to 1981, have had declining shares of the total immigrant PhDs. (Citizenship and Immigration Canada, 2003). Nearly 23 000 immigrants with PhDs came to Canada during the 10-year period prior to the 2001 Census. About 18 000 immigrant PhDs (78%) were science and engineering PhDs. The US share went from a high of 24.1% over the 1971-80 immigration period to a low of 5.9% over the 1991-2000 period while China's share went from a low of 2.4% to a high of 25.2% over the same immigration time periods (McKenzie, 2007). One of the main reasons for both the increases in immigrant PhDs, as well as the higher concentration of immigrant PhDs in science and engineering fields in that period, is due to the fact that Canada produced proportionately fewer graduates in mathematics, sciences and engineering than other G7 countries, with the exception of Italy according to 1997 OECD data. The bulk of Canada's recent immigrants with PhDs are not directly the result of foreign students remaining in Canada but rather from a combination of immigration policy changes in the early 1990s and market forces such as the high technology boom of the mid-to-late 1990s.

United States. In the United States, a similar trend can be seen. According to the National Science Board (2004) jobs requiring science and engineering skills in the American labour force is growing at almost 5% per year but the domestic supply of science and engineering graduates has not kept up with demand. Growth in the United States' science and engineering labour force has been maintained above the domestic supply of science and engineering graduates mainly because of the large number of foreign-born workers. Between 1990 and 2000, the share of US science and engineering occupations filled by scientists and engineers who were born abroad increased from 14% to 22% at all university and college degree levels. At the doctorate level the increase was from 24% to 38%, the highest increase of all university and college degree levels.

As a final note, relying extensively on international flows and mobility policies to fill existing or future gaps in the supply of HRST may provoke some imbalances, such as brain drain (OECD, 2008a). But it is not really the case for many large and more recent space-faring countries. Between 1978 and 2005, around 770 000 mainland Chinese went abroad to study, mainly in the United States, Japan and the United Kingdom; and according to Chinese statistics approximately 180 000 are estimated to have returned over that period (OECD, 2008e). As a result, those overseas returnees have founded many of the country's high-technology companies, and several are playing a prominent role in the Chinese space programme in 2011.

4. New technologies and innovative applications on the horizon

Developing a capable and sustainable space programme is a continuous process, as space agencies and industry all seek to improve existing systems and develop new ones. New technologies and innovative applications are therefore in development in major space-faring countries.

Forecasting the future of space applications

As part of its foresight mission, the OECD/IFP launched in 2002 a project to investigate the potential contributions of space applications in meeting five key societal challenges (*i.e.* the environment, use of natural resources, increasing mobility of people and goods, growing security threats, and the move towards the information society). The main challenges identified in this demand-based study remain prominent today and have even intensified in some cases. Scenarios were conducted, technology maps were drawn, and as a result, the contribution of space technologies was deemed to be significant in various potential futures, if a number of framework conditions were met. At the end of the exercise, following a large consultation with more than a hundred public and private organisations, a list of "promising space applications" was developed, with applications that were either already feasible or had a good chance of becoming so in the coming years (OECD, 2004, 2005).

> **Box 1.5. Space 2030 scenarios and their impacts on space technologies**
>
> Three scenarios came out of the OECD IFP *Space 2030* exercise, they are: *Smooth sailing* (multilateralism and international co-operation prevail, substantial progress generously diffused); *Back to the future* (more regionalisation, opposing geopolitical blocks; moderate economic growth in the West but substantial in the East; moderate technology progress subject to strategic diffusion) and *Stormy weather* (series of serious crises in international relations; rising tensions over resources; the environment sharply deteriorates in parts of the world). Not one of those scenarios is ideal. The three synthesis scenarios provide very different future visions of the world, ranging from the optimistic outlook of *Smooth Sailing*, which foresees advances to improve human conditions in a spirit of international co-operation, to the darker picture depicted by *Stormy Weather*, which sees a world where economic blocks disagree on how to deal with major problems facing humanity (*e.g.* conflicts, poverty, malnutrition, disease, environmental degradation). Even the more optimistic scenario is not without its darker side, notably the rise of non-state actors increasingly capable of using violence in the pursuit of their cause, whatever it may be. Despite these differences, the scenarios share some common ground with respect to their impacts on space:
>
> - Military space plays an important role in all three scenarios, although to different degrees. Even in the relatively peaceful world of *Smooth Sailing*, security concerns are high and a number of countries are anxious to strengthen their military space capability (*e.g.* earth observation satellites, telecom for the military). This results in a strong and robust demand for military and dual-use space assets worldwide. Almost ten years after the *Space 2030* exercise, many recent developments in military space systems seem to confirm this important trend.

> **Box 1.5. Space 2030 scenarios and their impacts on space technologies** *(cont.)*
>
> - Civil space also plays an important role in all scenarios, although for different reasons. In *Smooth Sailing*, its role in fostering international co-operation to solve world problems (education, health, and environment) is central. In *Back to the Future*, prestige projects and attempts to increase soft power give importance to spectacular ventures to the Moon or to Mars. Space is also called upon to solve world problems but in a less co-ordinated, more fragmented and less effective manner. Even in *Stormy Weather*, the outlook for civil space is not bleak, although the resources devoted to it may be quite small. As in the other scenarios, the development of dual-use technologies remains a priority; prestige and soft power are also important drivers. Important gains can still be made if space firms are able to demonstrate that space solutions can bring about major savings for cash-strapped governments.
>
> - Commercial space varies unsurprisingly more than military space across scenarios, as customers range from governments to retail consumers (*e.g.* satellite television users). Commercial applications thrive in the *Smooth Sailing* scenario, remain strong in the *Back to the Future* scenario, but are more constrained in the *Stormy Weather* scenario (international markets are smaller). It is worth noting that for many space firms, Scenario 2 may be the most favourable because of the protection it offers against competition from foreign firms. In all three scenarios, commercial space benefits from rising military budgets for space.

The promising applications range from traditional to less orthodox applications. The demand is based on social, governmental and commercial needs, but it is also affected by diverse factors (*e.g.* competition from terrestrial applications). Almost ten years after the exercise, a number of applications have become a reality, building on niches that few competitive terrestrial applications can fill (*e.g.* global view offered by satellites) and benefitting from the rapid uptake of information technologies by the general public (*e.g.* use of cell phones and the Internet). Already, in late 2010, several contenders have become full blown applications in a number of OECD countries, such as location-based consumer services. The day-to-day uses of GPS terminals and navigation tools in cell phones keep growing in many countries.

From demonstrations to new applications

A number of advances are expected in the classical sphere of space applications (telecommunications and navigation applications), where satellites could contribute to the further development of information systems and networks (*e.g.* more broadband to rural areas, high definition and 3D television, air traffic management). But in addition, several relatively new space systems could be moving from demonstrations to potentially routine systems in the next ten years, including Automatic Identification System (AIS) via satellite and space situational awareness (SSA).

Automatic Identification System (AIS) via satellite. This application is becoming very useful in the maritime transportation sector. Every ship-at-sea above 300 gross tonnes is currently required to carry an Automatic Identification System (AIS), an anti-collision system that allows countries to monitor ship traffic along their coasts by receiving continuous messages with the vessel's information and positioning. The development of micro-satellites dedicated to AIS, notably by Norway, has demonstrated that the AIS area coverage can expand significantly, making it easier to monitor ship traffic and fishing in the seas and oceans, not only in coastal areas. In January 2011, there are already five

> ### Box 1.6. **List of promising space applications**
>
> On the basis of three scenarios, a list of "promising applications" was developed:
>
> **Main contenders**
> - Distance learning and telemedicine (broadcasting to remote areas and across national borders, medical remote surveillance).
> - E-commerce (enabling changing work patterns due to mobile workforce/home working and economic consequences, HDTV teleconferencing).
> - Entertainment (digital radio, TV, data and multimedia broadcasting to fixed [less likely mobile] assets, high bandwidth to the home/convergence of different media).
> - Location-based consumer services (driver assistance and navigation aids, insurance based on real-time usage data, vehicle fleet management, asset tracking (especially high-value) and road repair management).
> - Traffic management (location and positioning of aircraft and ships, optimisation of airport traffic management, optimisation of traffic management – road pricing – driver behaviour logging).
> - Precision farming and natural resources management (precision agriculture for maximal efficiency in equipment and application of fertiliser, deforestation and forestry management).
> - Urban planning (plans, maps and numerical terrain models, precise positioning of engineering structures and buildings, automatic control of job site vehicles, management and optimisation of job site vehicle routes).
> - Disaster prevention and management (telecom capability in absence of ground infrastructure, remote assessment of damage and pollution for insurance claims).
> - Meteorology and climate change (meteorological and sea condition forecasting for commercial sea shippers, pollution maps with evolution in time, monitoring of the application of treaties, standards and policies).
>
> **Outsiders**
> - Adventure space tourism (suborbital then orbital).
> - Power relay satellites.
> - In-orbit servicing.

programmes underway and more are expected nationally and internationally over the coming years. They include: Kongsberg Defence and Aerospace (Norway), Luxspace (Luxembourg), ComDev (Canada), AprizeSat (the United States/Argentina) and Orbcomm (the United States). These AIS system will increasingly serve not only to ensure more efficient and secure ship traffic in the busiest international sea lanes, but contribute to track ships in the case of oil monitoring and illegal fishing.

Space situational awareness (SSA). Another example of new space application development concerns the growing capabilities of space situational awareness (SSA) systems. Using ground and space-based elements, SSA is a surveillance system developed originally as an early warning system for incoming ballistic missiles. But it serves also to track the trajectories of operational satellites and large space debris in orbit, as well as to give information on space weather (*e.g.* geomagnetic storms), which may affect satellites. Four countries have some level of SSA capabilities so far (France, Germany, the Russian Federation and the United States). As orbits get more crowded with operational and defunct satellites, recent incidents have brought more attention to the need to monitor growing space traffic (*e.g.* 2009 collision between a non-operational Russian satellite and a communications satellite). Taking into account security implications, international co-operation is increasingly envisaged to facilitate better monitoring and early warning for the numerous civilian, commercial and military space operators who have assets in orbit.

Old and new challenges

Despite new promising applications on the horizon, several challenges may dampen their growth: radio spectrum's growing scarceness, the high cost of access to space and the competition from terrestrial alternatives.

Ensuring access to radio spectrum and avoiding radio frequency interferences. Radio spectrum is a limited natural resource. Satellite communications, earth observation and navigation all share radio spectrum with a wide range of other ground-based systems, such as aircraft radars, cellular telephones and wireless Internet. Spectrum can be used actively (*i.e.* emitting a signal, whether purposefully or not, as in the case of a cellular telephone, wireless Internet or a garage-door) or passively (*i.e.* no signal or communication is transmitted, like antennas onboard satellites which only track naturally occurring signals for scientific purposes). As noted by the US National Research Council (2010), the explosive growth of the radio spectrum's commercial use over the past 20 years is starting to have strong impacts on many commercial and scientific projects. As an example, many space observatories around the world are significantly impeded or precluded by radio frequency interference, necessitating costly interference mitigation. Sharing spectrum could become less problematic in some cases, thanks to technical advances. But overall, this situation calls for more co-operation via ITU.

Accessing orbit more cheaply. Putting satellites in orbit is still a major and expensive feat that few countries can perform. Out of the 50 countries with satellites in orbit, only 10 possess the technologies to launch. In addition, to reach the most profitable and strategic orbits, only five countries and ESA so far, via the Ariane programme, have developed cryogenic rocket engine technology (*i.e.* the United States, the Russian Federation, France, Japan and China). This key technology contributes to launching heavier satellites and reaching high orbits, in particular in the geostationary arc (36 000 kilometres altitude), where profitable commercial telecommunications satellites and key meteorological satellites are placed. Other countries are actively pursuing that next step in space launcher technology, like India (ISRO, 2010).

But launching satellites in lower orbits remains a high-priced endeavour. Building on decades-long proven R&D, a number of recent operators are developing new launchers, such as SpaceX with its Falcon 9 programme. The objective is to offer governments and the commercial operators cheaper alternatives to launch their satellites, compared with the traditional providers in the space industry. In addition, more R&D is ongoing in different parts of the world to create the next generation of launchers. For example, as part of its responsive space doctrine, the United States Air Force is developing an unmanned reusable spaceplane, with the objective to offer faster and cheaper turnaround times and operations than traditional space rockets. A first mission of the X-37B prototype started in April 2010 with a successful landing in December, while a second prototype could fly in 2011 (Clarke, 2010). Following the experience of many other space technologies, this type of military-led R&D could lead in time to technology transfers towards the civilian and commercial space transportation sectors.

Innovative terrestrial alternatives. As a final challenge, the take-up of space applications may be challenged in some cases by the development of innovative terrestrial alternatives. Space solutions represent the only practical means to obtain telecommunications links or images from remote areas. But the competition with new and more affordable terrestrial alternatives is growing, particularly in telecommunications. The delivery of cable and fiber solutions, as well as new mobile networks, could impede the development of some commercial satellite applications in well connected urban areas in OECD countries. But this is also the case in non-OECD countries. As an example, the CAREN project in Central Asia aims to establish a high-capacity research and education network as a gateway to global research collaboration. A new broadband Internet network using terrestrial fiber is being considered for development as an alternative to the current Silk project's satellite system, to connect researchers, educators and students in Kazakhstan, Kyrgyzstan, Tajikistan, Turkmenistan and Uzbekistan (ITU, 2010).

References

Aerospace Industries Association (AIA) (2008), *Launching the 21st Century American Aerospace Workforce*, Aerospace Industries Association's National Security Council and the Industrial Base and Workforce Committee, Washington DC, December.

AeroStrategy (2009), *Aerospace Globalization 2.0: The Next Stage*, Washington DC, September.

Center for Earth Observation and Digital Earth (2010), *Employment: Team Profile*, CEODE, Beijing, www.ceode.cas.cn, August (in Chinese).

Chinese Academy of Sciences (2009), *China to 2050, Space Technology Development Roadmap*, Beijing, June (in Chinese).

Citizenship and Immigration Canada (2003), *Immigrant Occupations: Recent Trends and Issues*, Minister of Public Works and Government Services, Ottawa.

Clarke, S. (2010), "Atlas Rocket Delivers Air Force Spaceplane to Orbit", *Spaceflight Now*, 22 April.

Cohendet (2010), "Assessing Socio-economic Impacts of Space Projects: Lessons Learned and New Avenues of Research", OECD Workshop, "Valuing the Socio-economic Contributions of Space Applications", 23 September, Paris.

European Science Foundation (ESF) (2003), *Demography of Space Science*, ESF, Strasbourg.

Eurospace (2010), *Satellites Launch Database*, Paris.

Farrell, D. (2005), "China's Looming Talent Shortage", *The McKinsey Quarterly*, Vol. 4.

French, H.W. (2005), "China Luring Scholars to Make Universities Great", *New York Times*, New York, 28 October.

Gallagher, M. et al. (2009), *OECD Reviews of Tertiary Education: China, OECD Thematic Review of Tertiary Education*, OECD Publishing, Paris.

Gereffi, G. and V. Wadhwa (2005), "Framing the Engineering Outsourcing Debate: Placing the United States on a Level Playing Field with China and India", *Working Paper*, Duke University.

Goldman, C.A. (2008), *Education and the Asian Surge a Comparison of the Education Systems in India and China*, RAND Center for Asia Pacific Policy, Washington DC.

Goldstein, A. (2002), "The Political Economy of High Tech Industries in Developing Countries: Aerospace in Brazil, Indonesia and South Africa", *Cambridge Journal of Economics*, Vol. 26, No. 4, July.

Guillermard, V. (2009), "EADS lance des passerelles entre le spatial et la défense", *Le Figaro*, Paris, 14 March.

Indian Space Research Organisation (ISRO) (2010), "Flight testing of the Indigenous Cryogenic Stage in GSLV-D3 Mission not Successful", *ISRO Press Release*, Indian Space Research Organisation, Bangalore, 15 April.

International Telecommunications Union (ITU) (2009), *Confronting the Crisis: Its Impact on the ICT Industry*, ITU, Geneva, February.

ITU (2010), *Monitoring the WSIS Targets: A Mid-term Review*, World Telecommunication/ICT Development, Report 2010, International Telecommunications Union, Geneva.

Jaramillo, C. (ed.) (2010), *The Space Security Index*, Project Ploughshares, Waterloo, Ontario, Canada, August.

Lejeune, D. (2004), *La gestion des âges dans les industries aéronautiques et spatiales*, Inspection générale des affaires sociales, Report No. 004-052, Paris, May.

Maloney, P. and M. Leon (2007), "The State of the National Security Space Workforce", *Crosslink*, Vol. 8, No. 1, Spring.

McKenzie, M. (2007), "Where Are the Scientists and Engineers?", *Statistic Canada*, Science, Innovation and Electronic Information Division (SIEID), Montreal.

Metcalfe, T.S. (2008), "The Production Rate and Employment of Ph.D. Astronomers", PASP, 120, 229.

National Research Council (2007), *Building a Better NASA Workforce: Meeting the Workforce Needs for the National Vision for Space Exploration*, Space Studies Board, Aeronautics and Space Engineering Board, Washington DC.

National Research Council (2010), *Spectrum Management for Science in the 21st Century*, Committee on Scientific Use of the Radio Spectrum, Committee on Radio Frequencies, Washington DC.

National Science Foundation (2010), *Science and Engineering Indicators 2010*, Washington DC.

OECD (2003), *The Sources of Economic Growth in OECD Countries*, OECD Publishing, Paris.

OECD (2004), *Space 2030: The Future of Space Applications*, OECD Publishing, Paris.

OECD (2005), *Space 2030: Tackling Society's Challenges*, OECD Publishing, Paris.

OECD (2007), *PISA 2006: Science Competencies for Tomorrow's World*, Paris.

OECD (2008a), *Adjusting to the Global Competition for Talent*, Report from the *ad hoc* Working Group on Steering and Funding of Research Institutions (SFRI), DSTI/STP(2008)5, Paris, April.

OECD (2008b), "Encouraging Student Interest in Science and Technology Studies", *OECD Global Science Forum*, Paris.

OECD (2008c), *Export Credit Financing Systems in OECD Member Countries and Non-Member Economies*, OECD Publishing, Paris.

OECD (2008d), *The Global Competition for Talent: Mobility of the Highly Skilled*, OECD Publishing, Paris.

OECD (2008e), *OECD Reviews of Innovation Policy: China*, OECD Publishing, Paris.

OECD (2008f), *Space Technologies and Climate Change*, OECD Publishing, Paris.

OECD (2009a), *International Migration Outlook 2009*, OECD Publishing, Paris.

OECD (2009b), *Main Science and Technology Indicators*, OECD Publishing, Paris.

OECD (2009c), *OECD Economic Surveys: Russian Federation 2009*, OECD Publishing, Paris, February.

OECD (2009d), *OECD Patent Statistics Manual*, OECD Publishing, Paris.

OECD (2009e), *PISA 2006 Data Analysis Manuals*, Paris.

OECD (2009f), *Society at a Glance*, OECD Publishing, Paris.

OECD (2010), *OECD Economic Surveys: Israel 2010*, OECD Publishing, Paris, January.

Pain, N. (1997), "Export Performance and the Role of Foreign Direct Investment", *Working Paper*, NIESR, London.

Saxenian, A. (2005), "China", in Commander, S. (ed.), *The Software Industry in Emerging Markets*, Edward Elgar, Cheltenham, the United Kingdom.

Seth, A. (2009), "Employment and Funding in Astronomy", *Astro2010: The Astronomy and Astrophysics Decadal Survey, Position Papers*.

Shang, J.S. (2004), "Three Decades of Accomplishments in Computational Fluid Dynamics", *Progress in Aerospace Sciences*, Vol. 40, No. 3, April, pp. 173-197.

Tauri Group (2010), *Personal Spaceflight Industry Summary*, Report, Washington DC.

Williams, P.K.G. (2009), "Training the Next Generation of Astronomers", *Astro2010: The Astronomy and Astrophysics Decadal Survey, Position Papers*.

Willis (2009), "Market Capacity", *Space Insurance Insight*, 1st Quarter 2009.

II. READINESS FACTORS: INPUTS TO THE SPACE ECONOMY

1. Governmental budgets for space activities

2. Capital stocks: Space assets in orbit and on the ground

3. Human capital

This chapter examines the financial infrastructures and human capital necessary to engage in significant space activities. Governmental budgets for space activities are first analysed, using data from Government Budget Appropriations or Outlays for R&D (GBAORD), followed by public institutional space budgets. A closer look at capital stocks gives an indication of the investments engaged in space programmes by some countries. To close this chapter, human resources in the space sector are also examined.

II. READINESS FACTORS: INPUTS TO THE SPACE ECONOMY

1. Governmental budgets for space activities

National and other institutional budgets often contribute to the start-up and development of capital-intensive and high technology sectors such as space. This section provides details on two aspects of government budgets dedicated to space activities: 1) Civilian space programmes as presented annually in Government Budget Appropriations or Outlays for Research and Development (GBAORD); and 2) Public institutional space budgets, covering both civilian and military budgets.

Civilian space programmes in Government Budget Appropriations or Outlays for R&D (GBAORD)

Since the beginning of the space age, government support for research and development (R&D) in the space sector has been crucial for developing civilian systems and applications. An analysis of GBAORD trends shows that civil space-related R&D budgets of many countries have peaked in the early to mid-1990s then decreased or stagnated, except for the Russian Federation (Figure 1.1). This trend may not translate into less funding. In fact, as more government support has been devoted to overall R&D in the OECD area over the years (i.e. the total GBAORD for OECD countries has more than doubled since 1996), the share dedicated to space R&D has generally benefitted from extra funding. The OECD total for civil space-related R&D budgets was USD 18.355 billion in 2009 (in current USD PPP), with a few large countries dominating the total (Figure 1.2). G7 countries dominated many of the top positions, with the United States leading with a budget of USD 10.8 billion. Other countries with relatively high space R&D expenditures include the Russian Federation, Japan, France, Germany and Italy. In addition, many countries have developed dual-use and military space programme, which may fall in defence R&D budgets.

Methodological notes

GBAORD data are assembled by national authorities analysing their budget for R&D content and classifying these outlays by "socio-economic objective" on the basis of NABS 2007 (Nomenclature for the analysis and comparison of scientific programmes and budgets) (OECD, 2002). GBAORD data have the advantage of being timely and reflecting current government priorities. However, the data refer to budget provisions, not to actual expenditures, and the breakdown in socio-economic objectives brings some limitations (i.e. the "exploration and exploitation of space" category excludes military space programmes, which are included in a specific "defence" category). GBAORD data can provide trends, which can be usefully complemented by other data (e.g. institutional budgets). Current USD PPP have been used to make budgets comparable.

Source

OECD (2010), *Main Science and Technology Indicators Database*, www.oecd.org/sti/msti.

Further reading

OECD (2002), *Frascati Manual: Proposed Standard Practice for Surveys on Research and Experimental Development*, OECD Publishing, Paris.

Note

1.1 and 1.2: Non-OECD country.

Information on data for Israel: *http://dx.doi.org/10.1787/888932315602*.

II. READINESS FACTORS: INPUTS TO THE SPACE ECONOMY

1. Governmental budgets for space activities

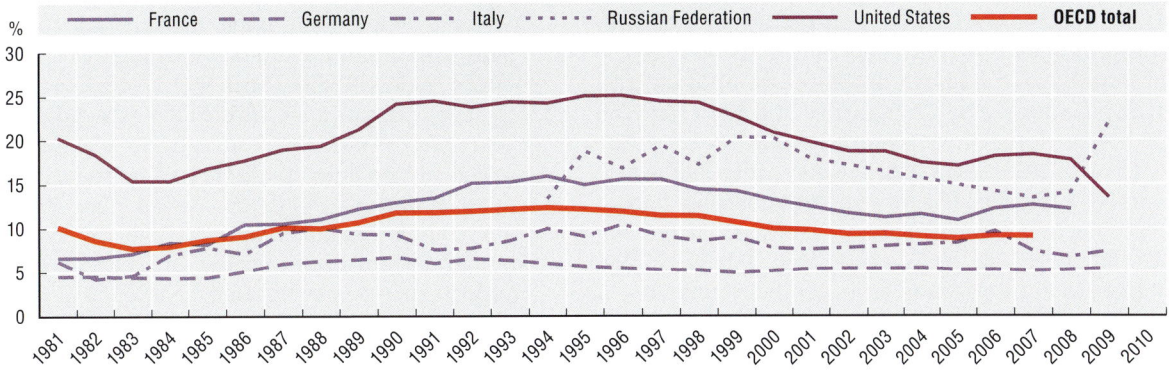

1.1 Civil space programmes as a percentage of civil GBAORD for selected countries
1981 to 2010 (or latest available year)

StatLink ⇒ http://dx.doi.org/10.1787/888932400247

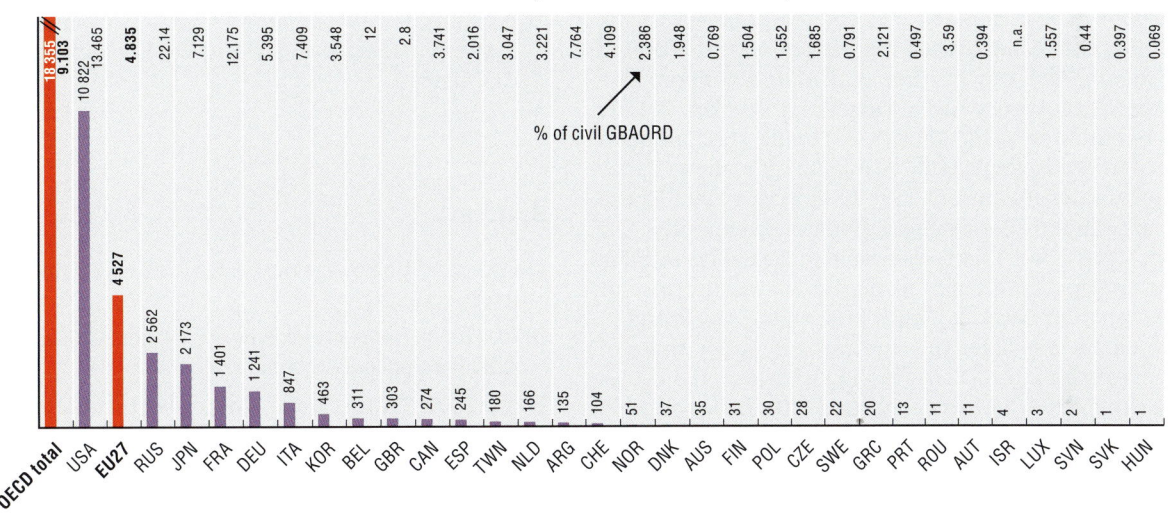

1.2 Civil space budget in Government Budget Appropriations or Outlays for R&D (GBAORD)
Current USD PPP million and as % of civil GBAORD, 2010 or latest year available

StatLink ⇒ http://dx.doi.org/10.1787/888932400266

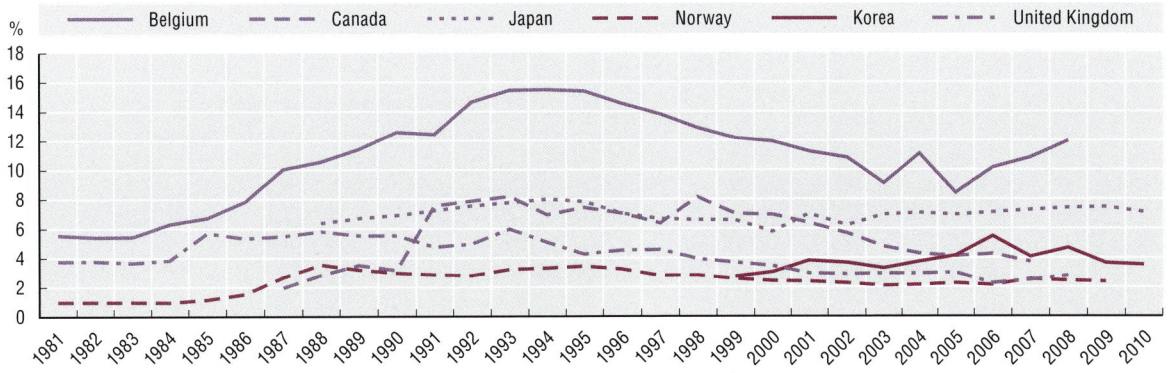

1.3 Civil space programmes as a percentage of civil GBAORD for selected countries
1981 to 2010 (or latest available year)

StatLink ⇒ http://dx.doi.org/10.1787/888932400247

II. READINESS FACTORS: INPUTS TO THE SPACE ECONOMY

1. Governmental budgets for space activities

National budgets for space

Since the first publication of *The Space Economy at a Glance* in 2007, the number of OECD and non-OECD countries with space programmes has continued to rise, as well as the governmental space budgets dedicated to military and civilian applications. The G7 countries still represent the bulk of institutional investments in space with some USD 53 billion in 2009, followed by the very active BRIC countries, with USD 9.6 billion (Figure 1.5). The total space budget of the 35 countries examined represents conservatively some USD 64.4 billion in 2009, and an estimated USD 65.3 billion in 2010 (see Section 1). Based on preliminary analysis, a number of countries have reduced their space budgets in 2010 because of budgetary measures (*e.g.* Greece, Spain), while others are investing more as part of their innovation and R&D strategies (*e.g.* France, Germany, India, the United States). Reduction or more modest increases are however expected in 2011 in most OECD and non-OECD countries, as the impacts of the economic crisis are reflected in governments' expenditures. Five countries have invested more than USD 2 billion in both 2009 and 2010 (the United States, China, Japan, France and the Russian Federation), with the United States leading the way at more than USD 43 billion. The European Space Agency had a budget of 3.59 billion in 2009 (EUR 3.74 billion in 2010) (Table 1.4). Finally, the European Union contributes about EUR 700 million annually to space activities, under its current 2007-13 financial plan. These funds, allocated to the general European Union budget by member states, are primarily dedicated to the Galileo satellite navigation programme and to the Global Monitoring for Environment and Security (GMES) programme. The trend in rising budgets translates in some cases in larger share of space investments in GDP (Figure 1.6). However, the evolutions in the space budget's share in GDP between 2005 and 2009 may be affected by both an increase/decrease of space budgets (*e.g.* the Russian Federation has tripled its space budget since 2003), but also by changes in GDP itself (*e.g.* India's GDP has grown on average 8.4% annually since 2004). Overall, space represents a very small share of GDP in the cases of both BRIC and G7 countries (between 0.001% and 0.002% of total GDP).

Methodological notes

Estimates were done using institutional sources for budget information and provide orders of magnitude, which may still underestimate the amounts devoted to space programmes worldwide, especially as fiscal years may be different from country to country. Looking at public budgets dedicated to space activities poses several methodological challenges. When they are available publicly, budgets may not necessarily match current expenditures. In addition, published budgets may not reveal large confidential segments of space programmes (*e.g.* for military purposes) and/or may be classified under other areas of government expenditure. The risk of double counting exists too, as a number of governments provide direct and indirect funding to space-related international organisations. Chinese figures are estimates based on recent investments and not official data. All values are converted in current USD and/or PPP using OECD databases for the currency exchange rates (national units per USD, monthly average) and World Bank databases for the GDP data.

Sources

European Space Agency (ESA) (2010), *Annual Report*, www.esa.int.

OECD (2010), *National Accounts at a Glance 2010*, www.oecd.org/statistics/nationalaccounts/ataglance.

World Bank (2010), *World Development Indicators Database*, http://data.worldbank.org.

Further reading

OECD (2007), *The Space Economy at a Glance 2007*, OECD Publishing, Paris.

OECD (2009), *Measuring Government Activity*, OECD Publishing, Paris.

Notes

1.5: Chinese data based on estimates.

1.6: Non-OECD countries. Chinese data based on estimates.

Information on data for Israel: http://dx.doi.org/10.1787/888932315602.

II. READINESS FACTORS: INPUTS TO THE SPACE ECONOMY

1. Governmental budgets for space activities

1.4 European Space Agency Budget, 2010

	EUR million	%		EUR million	%
France	681.4	18.2	Finland	18.8	0.5
Germany	625.8	16.7	Canada	20.8	0.6
Italy	370	9.9	Ireland	15.1	0.4
United Kingdom	254.7	6.8	Portugal	18.8	0.5
Belgium	160	4.3	Luxembourg	10.9	0.3
Spain	195.2	5.2	Greece	16.2	0.4
Netherlands	95.2	2.5	Czech Republic	10.2	0.3
Switzerland	91	2.4	Co-operating states	5.2	0.1
Sweden	53	1.4	European Union	754.8	20.2
Austria	50.6	1.4	Other	206.1	5.5
Denmark	30.7	0.8			
Norway	60.2	1.6	**Total**	**3 744.7**	**100**

Source: ESA (2010).

1.5 Space budgets of selected OECD and non-OECD countries, 2009
Current USD million

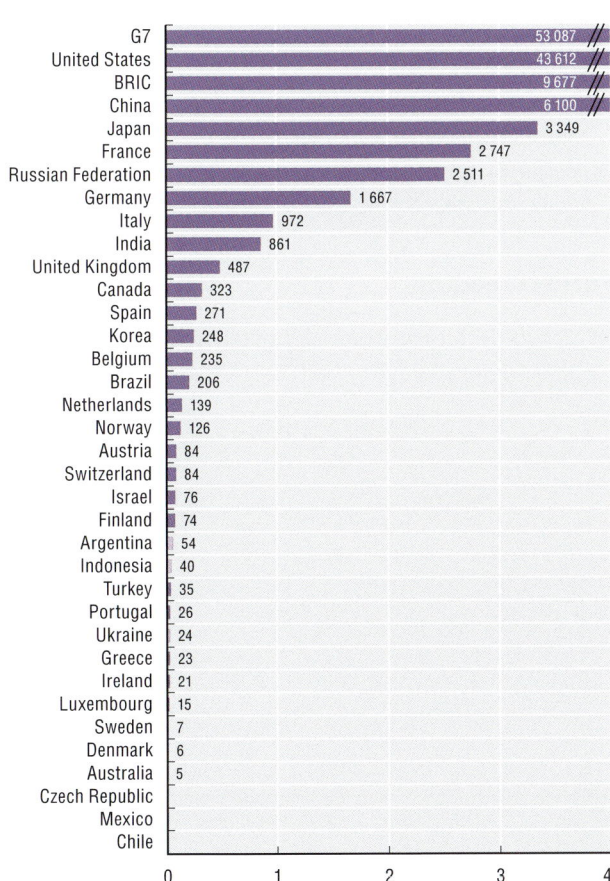

Source: OECD (2010) and World Bank (2010).

1.6 Space budgets of selected OECD and non-OECD countries as a share of GDP, 2005 and 2009
Percentage

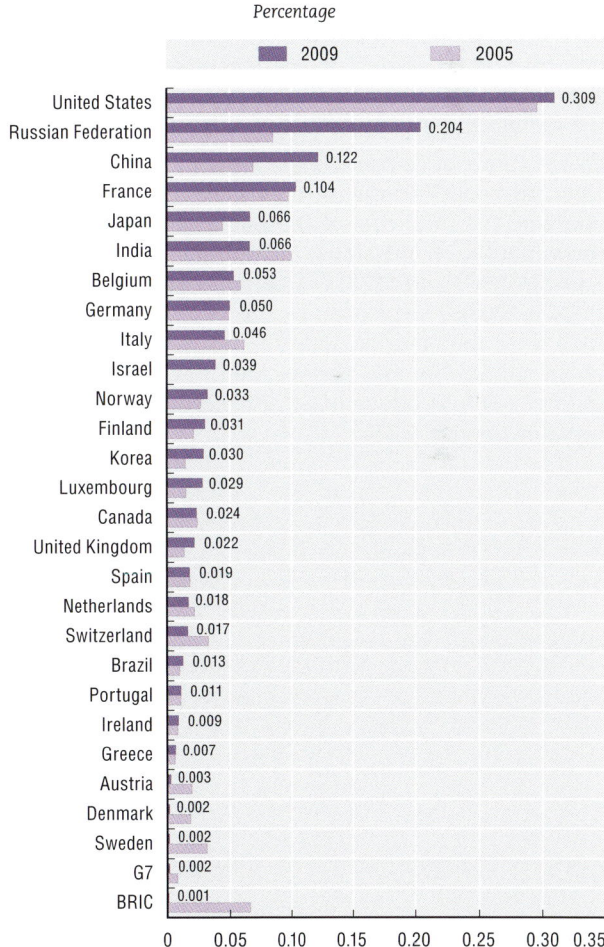

Source: OECD (2010) and World Bank (2010).

StatLink http://dx.doi.org/10.1787/888932400285

II. READINESS FACTORS: INPUTS TO THE SPACE ECONOMY

2. Capital stocks: Space assets in orbit and on the ground

Capital stocks represent the accumulation of equipment and structures available to produce goods or render services. In the case of space activities many of the installations are predominantly of a public nature (e.g. laboratories, launch pads) although the private sector has an increasingly important role in providing services. Because the sources are so diverse, capital stocks are difficult to estimate.

One approach is to use satellites as a proxy as discrete in-orbit assets. They can provide a measurable indication of the value of space infrastructure. In 2010, there were some almost a thousand active satellites in orbit with different governmental and commercial missions, of different sizes and planned lifetimes. Out of those satellites, the insurance market counts about 175 commercial satellites insured in orbit for a total value of some USD 170 billion (XL Capital, 2010).

Concerning physical infrastructures on the ground, a num-ber of countries are currently investing in setting up facilities for dedicated space centres. Table 2.1 provides an indication of the level of investments engaged by some countries when setting up space centres, ranging from a regional remote sensing centre to process satellite imagery to a full blown new spaceport to accommodate rockets.

There is more of course to a space programme than just its physical assets (e.g. satellites and launchers). As an example, the total cost of the Apollo programme, which encompassed 17 missions, including six lunar landings between 1960 and 1973, is estimated at USD 97.9 billion (in USD, 2008). The greatest capital stocks items (including R&D) were the Saturn V rockets (USD 6.4 billion) followed by the Command and Service Modules (USD 3.7 billion) and the Lunar Modules (USD 2.2 billion) (Congressional Research Service, 2009).

Methodological notes

The estimates provide mainly orders of magnitude. As in the case of other technology-intensive infrastructures, satellites are the visible outcomes of long term civilian and/or military R&D investments made by public investors, which are often not accounted for in the satellites' published costs. Sustained investments in scientific and technology fields are essential prerequisites for any active space-based infrastructure (i.e. from space launchers to in-orbit systems).

Sources

Congressional Research Service (2009), *The Manhattan Project, the Apollo Program, and Federal Energy Technology R&D Programs: A Comparative Analysis*, Report No. 7-5700 RL34645, June, www.crs.gov.

OECD (2010), *National Accounts at a Glance 2010*, www.oecd.org/statistics/nationalaccounts/ataglance.

XL Capital (2010), *Insurance Products: Space*, Bermudas, www.xlinsurance.com.

Further reading

OECD (2001), *Measurement of Capital Stocks, Consumption of Fixed Capital and Capital Services: OECD Manual*, Paris.

II. READINESS FACTORS: INPUTS TO THE SPACE ECONOMY

2. Capital stocks: Space assets in orbit and on the ground

2.1 Recent investments in ground-based infrastructures
National currencies

Infrastructure	Description	Investments (as of August 2010)
Vostochny Cosmodrome ("Eastern Spaceport") (the Russian Federation)	The spaceport is planned to replace the Baikonur site, for which the Russian Federation pays Kazakhstan USD 115 million a year for rent. The design and survey work for this large spaceport began in 2008, to be completed by 2015. Employing up to 30 000 people, the complex could occupy 550 km^2, 100 km from the border with China, with seven launch pads, including two for manned flights and two for cargo. The new facility should be in full mode by 2020.	RUB 400 billion (USD 13.9 billion). As of August 2010, some RUB 24.7 billion have been earmarked for the first three years of construction.
Sriharikota space centre extensions (India)	Development of a human capsule and related ground infrastructure, including a launch pad on Sriharikota Island (Bay of Bengal) and also an astronaut training facility in Bangalore. The first Indian orbital human mission could be launched in 2016.	INR 124 billion (USD 2.7 billion).
Soyuz launch complex (French Guiana)	In 2003, the Russian and French governments agreed to bring the new Soyuz 2 rockets to Kourou to diversify European/Russian launch offerings. The new complex includes a launch pad and a processing building for horizontal assembly of the Russian rocket, with four planned launches a year, the first one possibly in 2011.	Original investments of some EUR 344 million (including EUR 121 million investments by the company Arianespace) rising to EUR 405 million (USD 550 million).
Abu Dhabi space centre (United Arab Emirates)	Development of a 10 000 m^2 space complex, to receive and process imagery from diverse satellites, particularly the Italian Cosmo Skymed constellation.	USD 30 million as seed investment, funded by Abu Dhabi's Hydra Trading (a family consortium).
Mexico space centre (Mexico)	Development of a space center for the newly created Mexican space agency, at Quintana Roo (Chetumal) in the south of the country. The Center should be composed of one launch pad, a private airport runway, an astronaut training unit and a space museum.	MXN 120 million as seed investment (USD 9.7 million).

II. READINESS FACTORS: INPUTS TO THE SPACE ECONOMY

3. Human capital

The space sector comprises a myriad of specialised jobs, ranging from engineer to marketing specialists, although the majority of people working in the space sector have a science, mathematics, engineering or information technology background. Although estimates vary, existing data already provide some pointers as to the size of the workforce in the space sector, but not in the much wider space economy which includes more providers of space-related products and services. Overall, the space sector is traditionally not a very large employer. Less than 170 000 people work in space manufacturing in the United States, some 31 000 people in Europe and 50 000 in China. This is also a very concentrated industry, as for example, four large industrial holdings are directly responsible for more than 70% of total European space industry employment.

The dominant job categories in the space sector comprise engineers and technicians involved in designing, manufacturing and operating space and ground segments, but also information technology specialists. Scientists develop and test instruments that fly on satellites and probes, using the results in their various specialised fields (*e.g.* astronomy, astrophysics, astrobiology, atmospheric physics). There are also scientific-related jobs in applicative areas which use satellite data, for example in pollution monitoring and land mapping. Finally, administrative functions (accounting, legal, marketing) support institutional and commercial space programmes. Gender-wise, the proportion of women choosing science and technology (S&T) studies still remains below 40% in most OECD countries and this is reflected in the space industry. The choice of discipline is highly gender-dependant, and fields such as engineering or computing sciences remain largely male-dominated (OECD, 2008). Increasing the number of female students appears to be the most obvious way to increase the overall number of S&T students.

Methodological notes

Despite efforts to harmonise statistical information on education and employment at the international level, current data sets can still lead to conflicting interpretations. Key issues for the space sector include:

- *Sector of activity:* Statistics on space activities are usually embedded in larger aerospace and defence categories, making it challenging to separate the different activities. Statistics concerning defence personnel are especially challenging to obtain, particularly in non-OECD countries.
- *Counting time or people?* Countries may report employment in Full-time equivalents (FTEs) (counting shifts, not individuals) or numbers of persons employed.
- *Data sources:* Official employment statistics on the space sector, when they exist, often lack in quality and detail. To some extent, the gaps can be filled by non-official statistics, mainly from industry associations, which often focus on the space manufacturing industry while the larger services sector (*e.g.* professionals in satellite telecommunications) is not included, although increasingly private surveys try to cover the larger field of space applications.

Sources

Eurospace (2010), *The European Space Industry in 2009, Facts and Figures*, 14th Edition, Paris, August.

NASA (2010), *NASA Occupations*, Washington DC, http://nasajobs.nasa.gov/jobs/.

OECD (2008), *Encouraging Student Interest in Science and Technology Studies*, OECD Global Science Forum, Paris.

Further reading

British National Space Centre (BNSC) (2007), *Careers in Space: Opportunities in Space Science and Industry*, British National Space Centre, Department of Trade and Industry, London, March.

What is a space engineer?

There are many conflicting definitions of the engineering profession. Different statistical survey groups have adopted their own engineering classifications nationally and internationally. In the United States, the *National Center for Education Statistics* reports the total US engineering bachelor's degrees granted in 2004 to be 63 558. This number differs from the American Society of Engineering Education's 2004 statistic of 72 893, which has its own classification and categories for engineering graduates (Gereffi and Wadhwa, 2005). In China, the word "engineer" translates differently into various Chinese dialects and has no standard definition. Furthermore, Chinese provinces do not count degrees in a consistent way, as statistics may include degrees related to different disciplines (information technology and specialised fields such as shipbuilding). A motor mechanic or an IT technician could be considered an engineer, for example.

II. READINESS FACTORS: INPUTS TO THE SPACE ECONOMY

3. Human capital

3.1 Employment in space manufacturing in Europe
Full-time equivalent

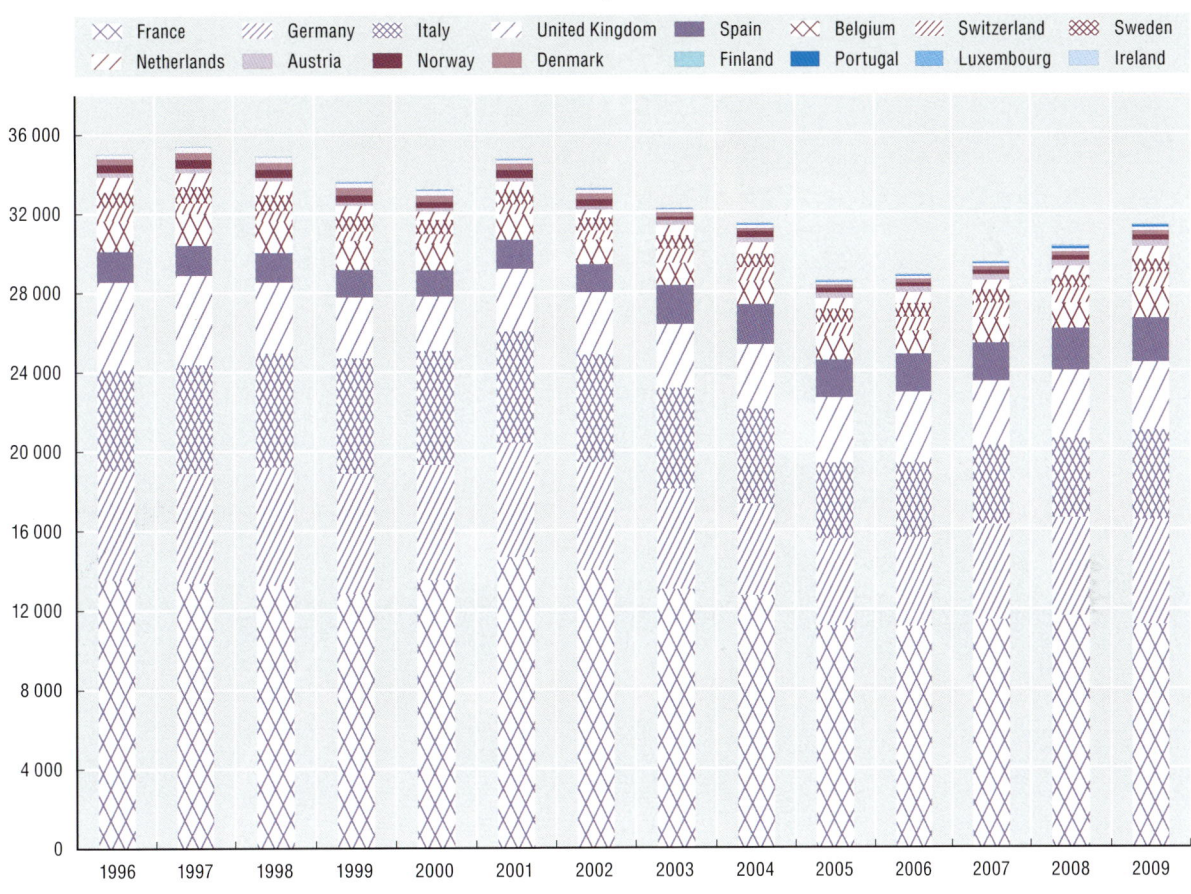

Source: Eurospace (2010).

StatLink ᔥ http://dx.doi.org/10.1787/888932400304

3.2 Examples of employment occupations at NASA

Category (% of NASA's positions)	Types of occupations
Professional, engineering and scientific (60%)	Occupations in this category require knowledge in a specialised field such as science, math, engineering, law or accounting (depending on the specific position). These positions generally require a bachelor's degree or higher degree with major study in a specialised field. This group covers positions such as: Accounting, Aerospace Engineering, Biology, Computer Engineering, Computer Science, General Engineering, Meteorology.
Administrative and management (24%)	Occupations in this category require knowledge of principles, concepts, and practices associated with organisations, administration or management. While these positions do not require specialised education (except for contracting positions), they do involve the type of skills (analytical, research, writing, judgment) typically gained through a college level education, or through progressively responsible experience. This group covers positions such as: Administrative Specialist, Budget Analyst, Contract Specialist, Information Technology Specialist, Public Affairs Specialist.
Technical and medical support (9%)	Occupations in this category support professional or administrative work. Duties require practical knowledge of techniques and equipment, gained through experience and/or specific training less than that represented by college graduation. This group covers positions such as: Electronics Technician, Engineering Technician, Meteorological Technician.
Clerical and administrative support (7%)	Occupations in this category provide general office or programme support duties such as preparing, receiving, reviewing, and verifying documents, processing transactions, maintaining office records, or locating and compiling data or information from files. This group covers positions such as: Accounting Technician, Clerk-Typist, Management Assistant, Office Automation Clerk, Procurement Clerk, Secretary.
Trades and labour (< 1%)	Occupations in this category include trades or crafts positions, including skilled mechanical and electrical crafts, and unskilled, semi-skilled, or skilled manual-labour occupations. This group covers positions such as: High Voltage Electrician, Instrument Maker, Model Making, Utility Systems Repair.

Source: NASA (2010).

III. INTENSITY: ACTIVITIES AND OUTPUTS IN THE SPACE ECONOMY

4. The manufacturing space industry
5. The satellite telecommunications sector
6. The satellite earth observation sector
7. Insurance market for space activities
8. International trade in selected space products
9. Innovation for future economic growth: Patents
10. Space launch activities worldwide
11. Space exploration activities

This chapter provides an overview of the activities derived from the space infrastructures, i.e. products or services that are produced or provided by the space sector. Outputs also include the benefits to industries or countries deriving from the production of space products or the performance of space-related R&D. These include financial benefits (e.g. trade revenues) and indicators of present and future financial benefits (e.g. patents).

III. INTENSITY: ACTIVITIES AND OUTPUTS IN THE SPACE ECONOMY

4. The manufacturing space industry

Space manufacturing remains a relatively small sector. According to industry reports, worldwide space manufacturing revenues increased from USD 10.5 billion in 2008 to at least USD 13.5 billion in 2009 (Satellite Industry Association, 2010) (Figure 4.1). This trend continued in 2010, as the main commercial satellite communications operators have been in the process of upgrading their fleet. Almost thirty contracts were signed in 2010 to order geostationary communications satellites. However based on other national and regional industry surveys, revenues generated by the construction of satellites and launchers, and their associated services, are probably larger worldwide. The space industries in India and China for instance provide a large amount of products and services to their growing national space programmes (see Chapter V).

Looking at two different actors in space manufacturing activities, Japan and Europe, important industrial differences in market structure appear. Japanese space industry sales totaled JPY 269 billion for the 2009 fiscal year (around USD 3.26 billion) and employed 6 300 workers (Figure 4.2). Sales have increased two years in a row in Japan, boosted by developments for the International Space Station and national launching capabilities. However, 92.6% of sales are driven by internal demand, the rest being exported. Based on orders, sales could amount to JPY 2.54 billion in 2010 and JPY 2.72 billion in FY2011, but a decrease in employment is still ongoing (SJAC, 2010). By comparison, as noted by Eurospace (2010), the European space industry faces an important level of exposure to international markets. Commercial and export sales represent 49.9% of revenues, compared with other countries which can rely more on their national institutional customers. Consolidated revenues for 2009 represented EUR 5.5 billion (around USD 7.5 billion), with 31 369 employees (Figure 4.3).

Methodological notes

National/regional industry associations use very diverse methodologies and statistical categories to collect data, which make international comparability challenging, although existing data provide interesting orders of magnitude. Eurospace, the Society of Japanese Aerospace Companies and the US Satellite Industry Association all conduct annual surveys of the space manufacturing industry. Since the first issue of *The Space Economy at a Glance* (2007), more data providers have made a move to make their data more transparent (*e.g.* mentioning current *versus* constant currencies, using inflation deflators). Efforts are also ongoing inside the International Astronautical Federation to discuss statistical methodological issues to promote and facilitate international data comparisons in the space community.

Sources

Eurospace (2010), *The European Space Industry in 2009, Facts and Figures*, 14th Edition, Paris, August.

Satellite Industry Association (2010), *State of the Satellite Industry Report*, Report prepared by Futron Corp., Washington DC, June.

Society of Japanese Aerospace Companies (SJAC) (2010), *Survey of the Japanese Space Equipment Industry*, SJAC, Tokyo (in Japanese).

Notes

4.1: Not adjusted for inflation, unconsolidated data. Based on other national and regional industry surveys, the revenues derived from space manufacturing could be much larger worldwide (see Chapter V with spotlight sections).

4.3: Includes human spaceflight and microgravity research.

III. INTENSITY: ACTIVITIES AND OUTPUTS IN THE SPACE ECONOMY

4. The manufacturing space industry

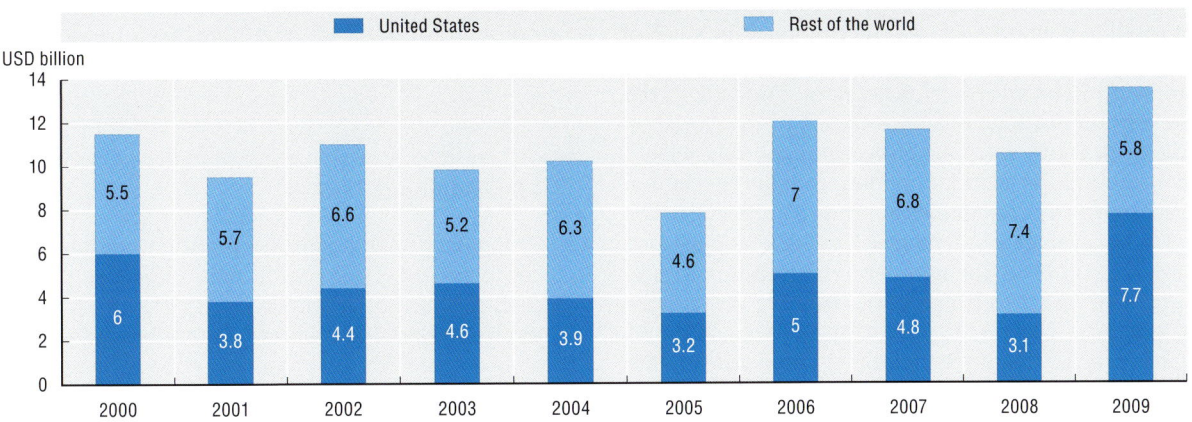

4.1 Estimates of space manufacturing revenues, 2000-09

Source: Satellite Industry Association (2010).

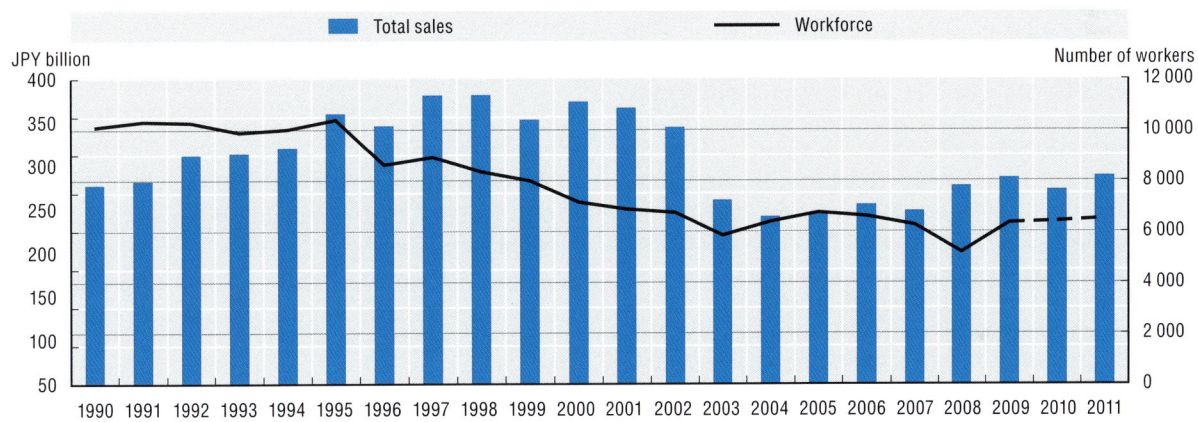

4.2 Consolidated sales and employment by Japanese space manufacturing companies

Source: SJAC (2010).

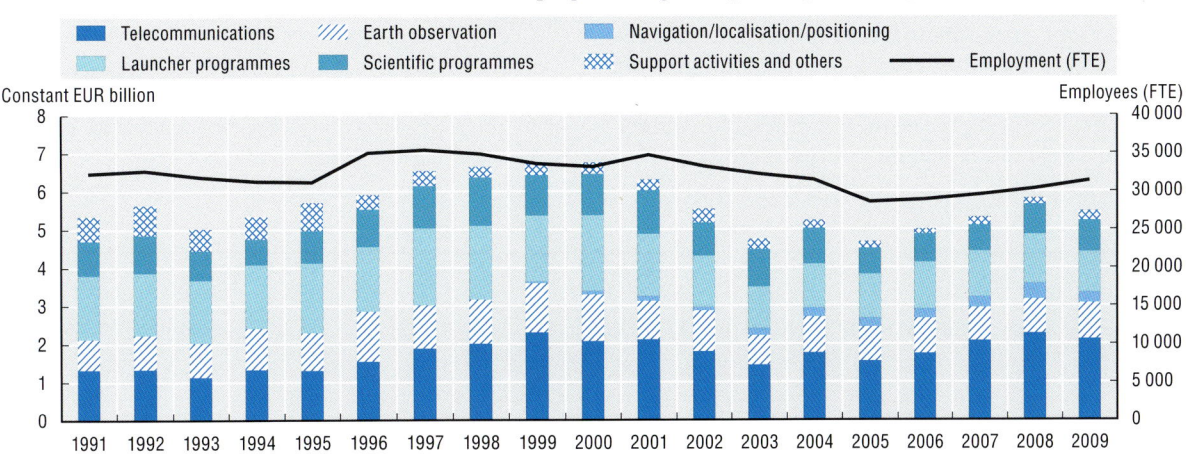

4.3 Consolidated sales and employment by European space companies

Source: Eurospace (2010).

THE SPACE ECONOMY AT A GLANCE 2011 © OECD 2011

III. INTENSITY: ACTIVITIES AND OUTPUTS IN THE SPACE ECONOMY

5. The satellite telecommunications sector

Satellite communications and broadcasting represent the most important space-related commercial market. Revenues of satellite operators are mainly generated by sales of capacity (i.e. leasing of satellite's transponders: data links and bandwidth) and added value services. The bulk of the satellite communications business comes from television. By early 2010, there were 1.4 billion households with a television around the world, providing roughly five billion people access to TV programmes at home (ITU, 2010). In the OECD, 95% on average of all households have at least one television (OECD, 2009). The number of households around the world with direct-to-home (DTH) satellite dishes rose from 82 million in 2000 to 177 million in 2008 (ITU, 2010). As shown in Figure 5.1 the number of direct broadcast satellite (DBS) subscribers outnumbers the numbers of terrestrial and cable broadcast viewers in 11 countries (particularly Austria, New Zealand, Germany and Ireland). DBS has already penetrated the mobile market particularly in Japan and Korea, as users can subscribe to satellite services and watch TV programmes using a mobile handset. Overall, the revenues generated by satellite telecommunications transmissions are estimated at more than USD 70 billion in 2010 (World Teleport Association, 2010). The delivery of multi-channel television via satellite has spread rapidly over the last decade, with 113 satellite operators worldwide, beaming over 15 000 channels to more than 130 million subscribers in over 85 countries (Northern Sky Research, 2010). As a result of mergers in the early 2000s, four operators (Intelsat, SES, Telesat and Eutelsat) account for about 75% of the global fixed-satellite services business worldwide with revenues estimated from USD 10 to almost 15 billion, depending on the source (Figure 5.2). In 2010, records were broken in revenue generation, despite the economic crisis, as the end-customers were relatively unaffected (i.e. the general public still watched television, the military still needed to communicate, ships at sea were still required to send data via satellites). In addition to satellite operators, the revenues of operators of very small aperture terminals (VSAT) networks grew 30% between 2006 and 2008, to about USD 3.7 billion (Comsys, 2010). One key driver comes from government-funded projects to guarantee universal access to the telecommunications grid for rural communities in South America, Africa and Asia. Showing resilience during the economic crisis, demand for satellite communications should continue growing over the next couple of years in both OECD and non-OECD countries boosted by increased numbers of users in mobile telephony, broadband, and high-definition and 3D TV programming.

Methodological notes

The satellite telecommunications' value chain is complex. This is also reflected in the data presented in this section, with estimates coming from both public and private sources (e.g. market surveys).

Sources

Comsys (2010), *Annual VSAT Report*, 11th Edition, Report prepared by Simon Bull, Comsys, London, January.

International Telecommunications Union (ITU) (2010), *Monitoring the WSIS Targets: A Mid-term Review*, World Telecommunication/ICT Development, Report 2010, International Telecommunications Union, Geneva.

Northern Sky Research (2010), *Global Direct to Home (DTH) Markets, 3rd Edition*, Washington DC, September.

OECD (2009), *OECD Communications Outlook 2009*, OECD Publishing, Paris.

Satellite Industry Association (2010), *State of the Satellite Industry Report*, Report prepared by Futron Corp., Washington DC, June.

Further reading

OECD *Information Technology Outlook*, Annual Report, www.oecd.org/sti/ito.

Notes

5.1: Japanese terrestrial subscribers are not included because DBS statistics were higher than total households with television sets. This is due to the inclusion of mobile television subscriber data.

5.2: Not adjusted for inflation.

III. INTENSITY: ACTIVITIES AND OUTPUTS IN THE SPACE ECONOMY

5. The satellite telecommunications sector

5.1 Breakdown of television access by distribution type: Terrestrial, cable, direct broadcast satellite
2006 or latest year, percentage of households with a television

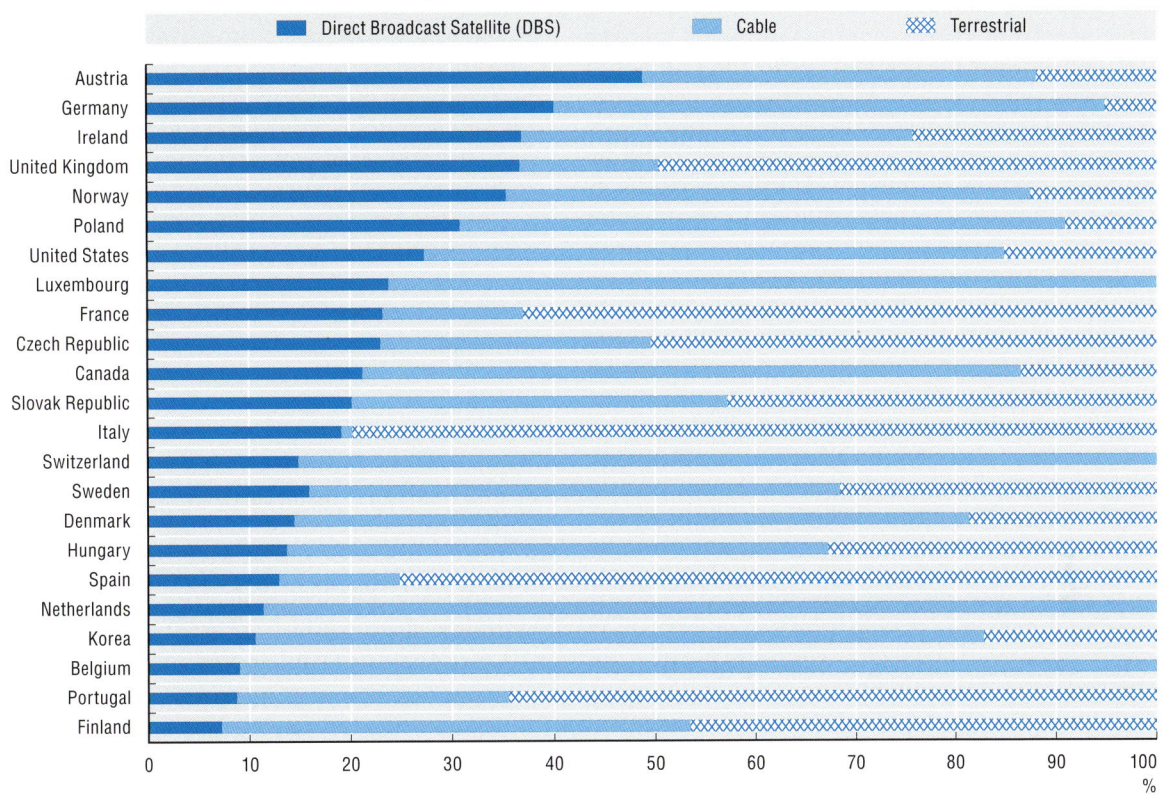

Source: OECD (2009).

5.2 Estimates of satellite communications and broadcasting revenues (2004-09)

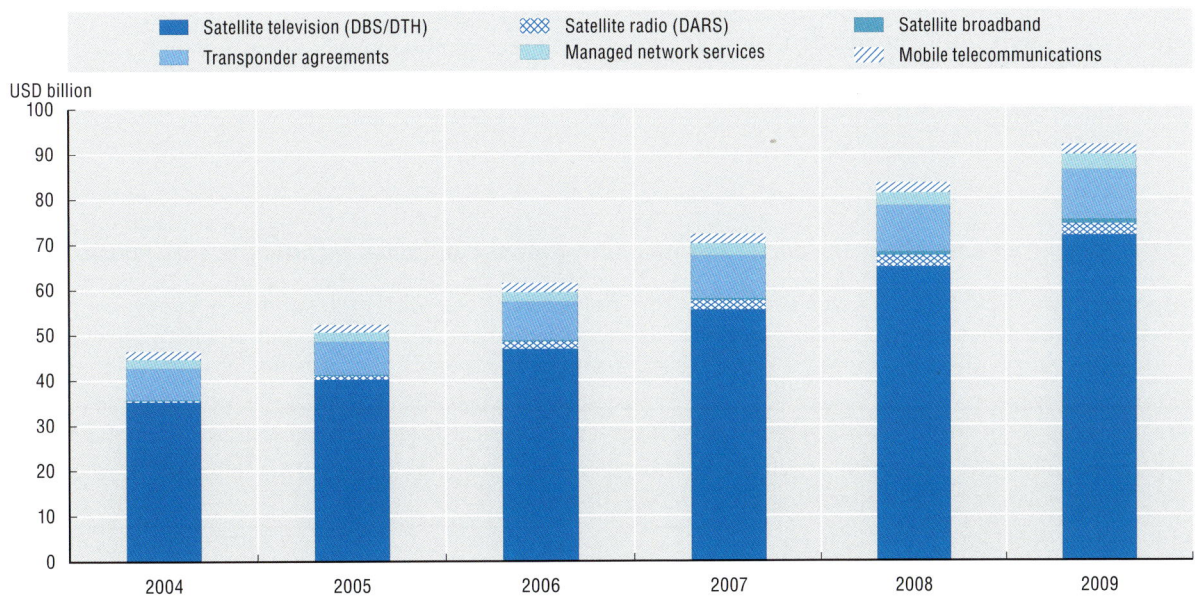

Source: Satellite Industry Association (2010).

III. INTENSITY: ACTIVITIES AND OUTPUTS IN THE SPACE ECONOMY

6. The satellite earth observation sector

Earth observation represents one of the earliest uses of space technologies. It allows the measurements from orbit of a very wide range of geophysical parameters, spanning the whole spectrum of the environment, including the atmosphere, land, oceans, ice and snow. The number of remote sensing satellites had been increasing as countries around the world seek to develop autonomous capabilities. Actors-wise, the United States, Europe, China and India are all important operators of satellite remote sensing fleets (Table 6.2). Out of the 109 operational earth observation missions managed by civilian space agencies, fifty are dedicated to gathering multi-purpose land imagery (CEOS, 2010). Commercial satellite earth observation represents a niche market valued at some USD 900 million to USD 1.2 billion in 2009, depending on the source, and includes full lines of products and services, not only imagery (Figure 6.1). The international commercialisation of satellite imagery started when restrictions on space technologies were relaxed at the end of the cold war. The main customers remain governmental agencies, which provide anchor contracts to remote sensing satellite operators in some cases. For example in 2010, the US National Geospatial Intelligence Agency launched a USD 2.8 billion Service Level Agreement ("EnhancedView SLA") to receive high-resolution earth imagery products and services over ten years from Digital-Globe, a commercial operator. According to Euroconsult estimates (2010), some 260 earth observation and meteorology satellites could be launched in the next ten years, generating USD 27.4 billion in manufacturing revenues for the space industry, compared to 128 satellites and USD 20.4 billion in revenues the previous decade. Although, it is estimated that 77% of all new earth observation satellites in the coming ten years will be owned or operated by a government or military entity, confirming the dominance of public institutions on the supply side (Northern Sky Research, 2010). In addition, more than a dozen radar satellites, which allow to see through clouds, are expected to be launched over the next decade.

Methodological notes

Data used here come from private data providers and from the Satellite database maintained by the Committee on Earth Observation Satellites (CEOS), an international group which aims to co-ordinate civil space-borne earth observations (i.e. fifty members and associate members made up of space agencies, national and international organisations). The CEOS database is updated annually, based on a survey of the organisation's members.

Sources

Committee on Earth Observation Satellites (CEOS) (2010), *CEOS Missions, Instruments and Measurements Database*, www.ceos.org.

Euroconsult (2010), *Satellite-Based Earth Observation, Market Prospects to 2018*, Paris.

Northern Sky Research (2010), *Global Satellite-Based Earth Observation*, 2nd Edition, November.

Satellite Industry Association (2010), *State of the Satellite Industry Report*, Report prepared by Futron Corp., Washington DC, June.

Notes

6.1: Not adjusted for inflation.

6.2: Several countries and agencies can co-operate for one satellite mission. Planned missions: Includes missions, both approved and under consideration, to be flown in the next two to ten years. Instruments: Earth observation satellites usually carry several instruments (*e.g.* diverse sensors) which can be built by agencies, laboratories, universities and/or industry.

Essential measurements about the earth and its environment conducted by satellite earth observations

Atmosphere: Aerosol properties, atmospheric humidity fields (water vapour), atmospheric temperature fields (air temperature), atmospheric winds, cloud properties, lightning detection, liquid water and precipitation rate, ozone, earth radiation budget (including solar irradiance), trace gases (carbon dioxide, methane and other greenhouse gases).

Land: Landscape topography (lake areas and levels), multi-purpose imagery (land cover, urban planning), soil moisture, surface temperature (fire disturbance), vegetation (biomass, agricultural crop identification), albedo and reflectance.

Ocean: Ocean colour (for biological activity, including fisheries), ocean salinity, ocean surface winds, sea level, currents, ocean wave height and spectrum, sea surface temperature.

Snow and ice: Ice sheet topography (glaciers and ice caps), sea ice cover, edge and thickness, snow cover, edge and depth.

Gravity, magnetic and geodynamic measurements: Groundwater, sea level.

III. INTENSITY: ACTIVITIES AND OUTPUTS IN THE SPACE ECONOMY

6. The satellite earth observation sector

6.1 Estimates of commercial remote sensing revenues, 2004-09
USD billion

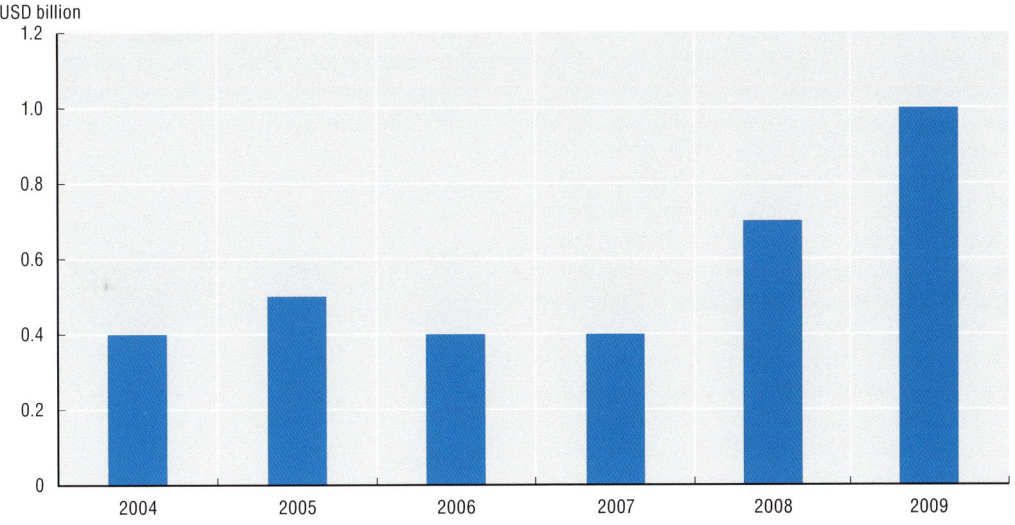

Source: Satellite Industry Association (2010).

6.2 Selected ongoing and planned earth observation missions by civilian agencies
As of October 2010

	Agency	Ongoing missions	Planned missions	Instruments
Argentina	CONAE	8	1	24
Brazil	INPE	3	6	11
Canada	CSA	6	6	11
China	CAST	3	7	35
	CRESDA	2	3	–
	NRSCC	8	16	22
Europe	EC	–	14	8
	ESA	11	28	51
	EUMETSAT	6	14	14
France	CNES	14	10	40
Germany	DLR	5	3	9
India	ISRO	12	15	36
Italy	ASI	13	5	16
Japan	JAXA	6	11	16
	JMA	2	–	4
Korea	KARI	2	4	8
Nigeria	NASRDA	1	2	3
Norway	NSC	1	–	1
Russian Federation	ROSHYDROMET	2	12	33
	ROSKOSMOS	3	13	40
South Africa	SANSA	1	–	1
Spain	CDTI	3	1	3
Sweden	SNSB	1	–	4
Thailand	GISTDA	1	–	2
Turkey	TUBITAK	1	–	2
United States	NASA	14	31	81
	NOAA	22	12	55
	USGS	2	1	5
Ukraine	NSAU	1	–	5
United Kingdom	UKSA	4	–	8

Source: CEOS (2010).

III. INTENSITY: ACTIVITIES AND OUTPUTS IN THE SPACE ECONOMY

7. Insurance market for space activities

Although launching satellites appears to be a routine operation to the general public, there are still major risks involved. A branch of the insurance sector specifically covers the commercial space sector's operations. The main risks covered still tend to be a failure at launch or mechanical troubles for telecommunications satellites (with different types of satellite insurance coverage) (Table 7.1). If losses occur, they tend to happen 83% of the time in the very first phases of the space systems' lifetime, either because of a malfunction of the rocket during launch or because of a satellite's breakdown during the first month of operations (Figure 7.2). The space insurance industry generates around USD 750 to USD 800 million a year. After several rocket failures in 1998 and 2001, in recent years space insurers have seen their profits rise and have lowered premium rates. Premium rates paid by satellite operators depend mainly on the reliability over time of the launch vehicles and satellite platforms they use. There are still relatively few satellites insured compared to the mass sent to orbit every year, some 40 per year out of the hundred launched every year (Figure 7.3). In 2010, out of the almost 1 000 operational satellites in orbit, about 175 commercial satellites are insured for a total value of some USD 170 billion (XL Capital, 2010). Approximately 36 commercial launches carrying 23 GEO satellites and 25 LEO satellites could be insured each year through 2013. Five operators have nearly 50% of the in-orbit fleet, and 48 operators split the remainder. In addition to insuring commercial satellites, two new segments for space insurance could develop over the next decade: space tourism via suborbital trips, and commercial flights of goods and provisions to the international space station. The insurance market traditionally thrives on volume. So as long as these potential future activities remain niche markets, premiums rates and possible exclusions will remain high (Pagnanelli Risk Solutions, 2009).

Methodological notes

Data are provided by insurers in constant USD.

Sources

Pagnanelli Risk Solutions (2009), "Space Activities and Relevant Insurance Implications", *Risk Management*, No. 45, May.

XL Capital (2010), *Insurance Products: Space*, Bermudas, www.xlinsurance.com.

Further reading

OECD work on insurance, www.oecd.org/insurance.

III. INTENSITY: ACTIVITIES AND OUTPUTS IN THE SPACE ECONOMY

7. Insurance market for space activities

7.1 Types of satellite insurance coverage

Launch – physical damage	Coverage for the spacecraft, launch system and any additional costs from intentional ignition of the launch vehicle until spacecraft separation.
Launch – post-separation	Included as an additional coverage to launch, provides for the full deployment and operation of the satellite from separation from launch vehicle until satellite reaches its intended orbital position through in-orbit testing.
In-orbit operations	Protects against the risk of a complete or partial failure of the satellite while operating in space.
Transponder coverage	Provides protection against the loss of one or more transponders being used on an operating satellite.
Satellite incentive coverage	Protects satellite manufacturers against loss of incentive payments due to lack of guaranteed performance of a satellite.
Launch risk guarantee	Provides for the full (or partial) cost for another launch if the satellite fails to reach its intended orbit, is destroyed, or if its functions are impaired resulting from a launch vehicle malfunction.

7.2 Occurrence of satellite's failures during first year of operations

Based on the number of insured satellites during the 2000-09 period

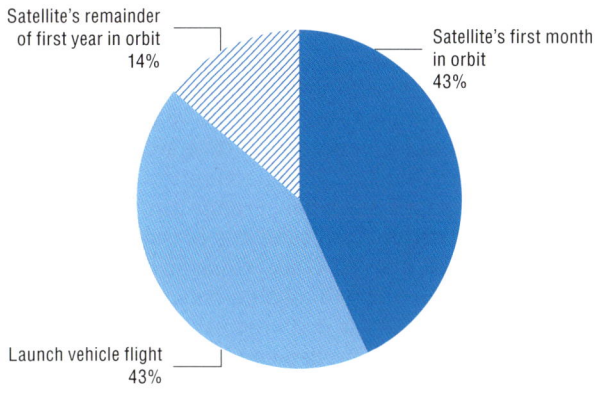

- Satellite's remainder of first year in orbit: 14%
- Satellite's first month in orbit: 43%
- Launch vehicle flight: 43%

7.3 Estimates on the number of satellites insured (1994-2013)

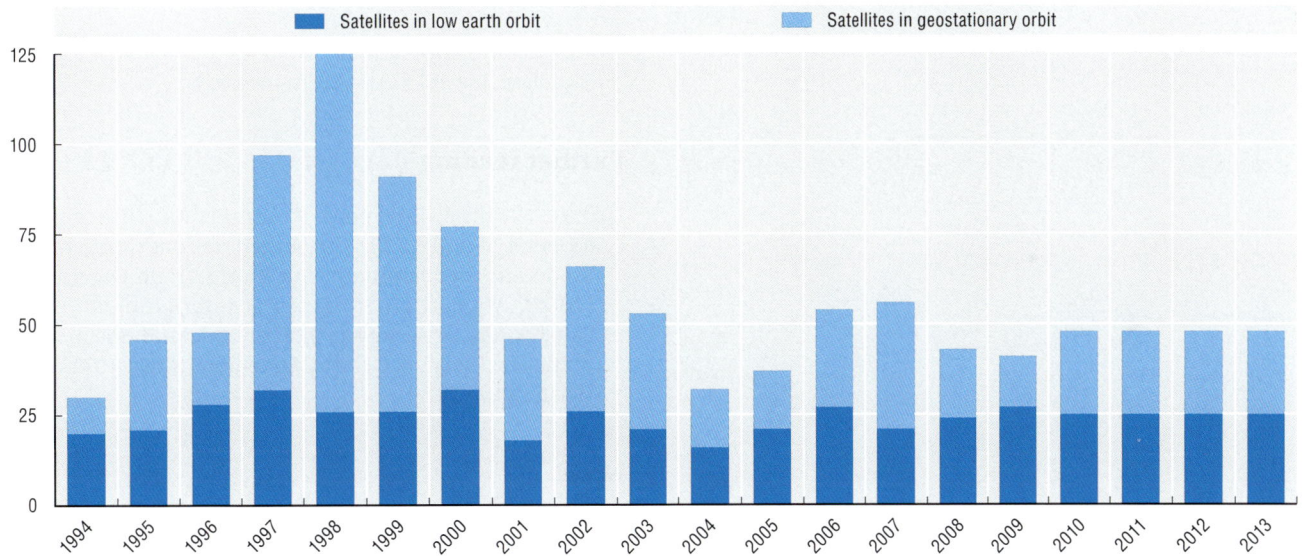

THE SPACE ECONOMY AT A GLANCE 2011 © OECD 2011

III. INTENSITY: ACTIVITIES AND OUTPUTS IN THE SPACE ECONOMY

8. International trade in selected space products

Not many space products and services are fully commercial, as most are strategic in nature and not freely traded. This section provides a partial overview of existing trade data by examining the exports of one commodity code with significant space components from the International Trade in Commodity Statistics (ITCS) database. Based on available trade data, Table 8.1 and Figure 8.3 show France, the United States, Belgium, Italy and Germany leading the exports of spacecraft (including satellites) and spacecraft launch vehicles. Concerning importers, a diversity of OECD and non-OCDE countries appear, reflecting the emergence of new actors in space activities. France and Luxembourg, homes of large commercial satellites telecommunications operators (Eutelsat and SES Global respectively) show a level of imports corresponding to satellite orders (*i.e.* commercial communication satellite's costs represent usually USD 150 to 300 million). Malaysia also shows an import of some USD 189 million in 2009, which could correspond to the launch that year of its first earth observation satellite and associated services.

Methodological notes

The data come from the International Trade by Commodity Statistics (ITCS) database jointly managed by the OECD and the United Nations. The Commodity Code used is 7925 "Spacecraft (including satellites) and spacecraft launch vehicles". Due to confidentiality, countries may not report some of its detailed trade, and imports reported by one country may not coincide with exports reported by its trading partners. Differences are due to various factors including national trade valuation (imports/exports including or excluding "cost, insurance and freight"), differences in inclusions/exclusions of particular commodities, or timing. These data need to be completed by industry association's results, as many of the space manufacturing contracts do not appear readily in official statistical databases.

Source

OECD (2010), *International Trade by Commodity Statistics Database*, www.oecd.org/std/trade-goods.

Further reading

United Nations, European Commission, International Monetary Fund, OECD, the United Nations Conference on Trade and Development and World Trade Organization (2002), *Manual on Statistics of International Trade in Services*, UN Department of Economic and Social Affairs Statistics Division, Geneva, Luxembourg, New York, Paris, Washington DC.

Note

Information on data for Israel: http://dx.doi.org/10.1787/888932315602.

III. INTENSITY: ACTIVITIES AND OUTPUTS IN THE SPACE ECONOMY

8. International trade in selected space products

8.1 Exporters of spacecraft (including satellites) and spacecraft launch vehicles
Current USD million in 2007, 2008 and 2009

	2007	2008	2009
Belgium	–	–	292
Brazil	34	9	1
Canada	1	1 699	–
France	614	360	1 768
Germany	258	–	185
India	–	1.1	0.6
Israel	–	328	–
Italy	–	90	249
Japan	0.2	–	–
South Africa	0.03	25	1.2
United Kingdom	–	217	8
United States	667	0.7	151
Others	5	0.7	11

8.2 Importers of spacecraft (including satellites) and spacecraft launch vehicles
Current USD million in 2007, 2008 and 2009

	2007	2008	2009
Canada	0.09	0.51	0.014
France	160.01	215.12	–
Germany	–	59.21	–
India	–	–	0.91
Japan	13.96	0.10	–
Luxembourg	218.11	218.52	–
Malaysia	–	–	189.49
Nigeria	–	–	0.12
Norway	0.29	–	0.05
Singapore	0.021	–	1.44
Sudan	5.63	165.18	–
Sweden	0.63	0.38	–
United Kingdom	0.42	–	–
United States	78.98	33.96	–
Others	0.33	0.41	0.16

8.3 Top exporters of satellites and launch vehicles in 2009
Current USD million

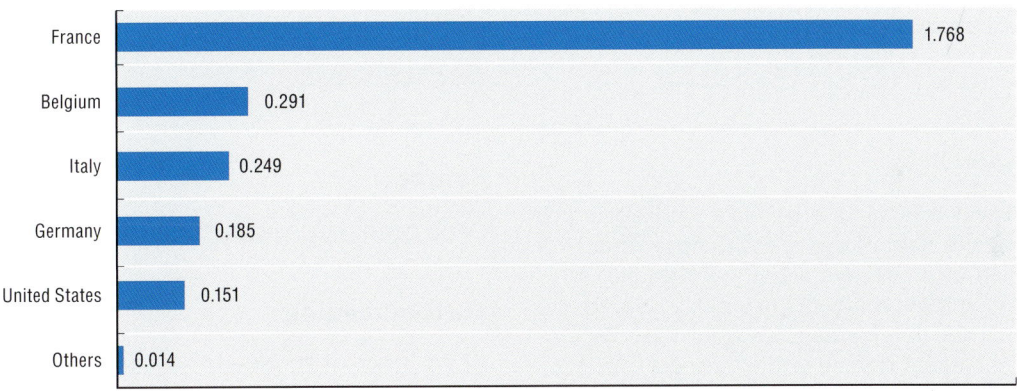

StatLink http://dx.doi.org/10.1787/888932400323

THE SPACE ECONOMY AT A GLANCE 2011 © OECD 2011

III. INTENSITY: ACTIVITIES AND OUTPUTS IN THE SPACE ECONOMY

9. Innovation for future economic growth: Patents

The space sector has often been considered one of the main frontrunners of technological development. This was evident at the beginning of the space age (1950s) which yielded pioneering space systems. Analysis of patents provides some insight into innovative activities concerning the electrical and mechanical machinery and equipment required for space-based systems (satellites, launchers) as well as the downstream applications, such as telecommunications navigation systems. The number of space-related patents has almost quadrupled in fifteen years when looking at the applications filed under the Patent Co-operation Treaty (PCT) (Figure 9.1). The downturn after 2002 is due to a large degree to time-lag effects described in the "Methodological notes". The narrow classification B64G: "Cosmonautics; vehicles or equipment thereof" shows a slower increase in the number of patents, meaning that other categories dealing with downstream products and services have gained in importance (Figure 3.6b and 9.2). The countries' share in space-related patents over the 2000-08 period shows the United States and Europe leading, followed by Korea and Japan (Figure 9.3). Finally, in terms of revealed technological advantage, eight countries demonstrate a level of specialisation in space technologies patenting. The Russian Federation, France, Israel and the United States show a large amount of patenting in space activities, compared to other economic sectors (Figure 9.4).

include space-related patent applications filed under the Patent Co-operation Treaty (PCT). The PCT offers applicants the possibility to seek patent rights in a large number of countries by filing a single international application with a single patent office (receiving office). Data on the number of PCT patent applications are more internationally comparable because they avoid home country advantages and cover inventions that are potentially worth patenting in more than one country. A methodological issue concerns the visible downturn of patent applications after 2001. This is mainly due to delays in updating patent databases and also the time-lag at the USPTO between the application of a patent and its granting. Thus, the downturn should not be misconstrued as a recession in terms of space-related patenting activities. Finally, the "revealed technological advantage" (RTA) index is defined as a country's share in patents in a particular field of technology, divided by the country's share in all patents. The index is equal to zero when the country holds no patents in a given sector, is equal to 1 when the country's share in the sector is equal to its share in all fields (*i.e.* no specialisation), and grows when a positive specialisation is found.

Methodological notes

Not all innovations are subjected to patenting processes. In the field of space technology under-representation of innovative activity within patent systems may be more marked since much dual-use space research and development is subject to secrecy. Space-related patents were identified using a combination of codes from the International Patent Classification (IPC) and key words searches in the patent title. The classification B64G: "Cosmonautics; vehicles or equipment thereof" was used as a starting point. It covers a large array of space-related systems and applications (including satellites; launchers; components; radio or other wave systems for navigation or tracking; simulators). In this analysis no adjustments have been made for inventions filed at both European Patent Office (EPO) and the United States Patent and Trademark Office (USPTO), although the results also

Source

OECD (2010), *OECD Patent Database*, August.

Further reading

OECD (2009), *OECD Patent Statistics Manual*, OECD Publishing, Paris.

OECD work on patent statistics, *www.oecd.org/sti/ipr-statistics*.

Notes

9.2: Partial information on EPO and PCT patents is available for priority year 2008. Partial information on USPTO patent grants on the whole period.

9.4: Partial information is available for priority year 2008. Only countries/economies with more than 1 000 PCT patents over the 2000-08 period (all sectors included) are included in the figure.

Information on data for Israel: *http://dx.doi.org/10.1787/888932315602*.

III. INTENSITY: ACTIVITIES AND OUTPUTS IN THE SPACE ECONOMY

9. Innovation for future economic growth: Patents

9.1 Evolution of space-related patents (1980-2007)
Number of patents filed by patent offices and priority date

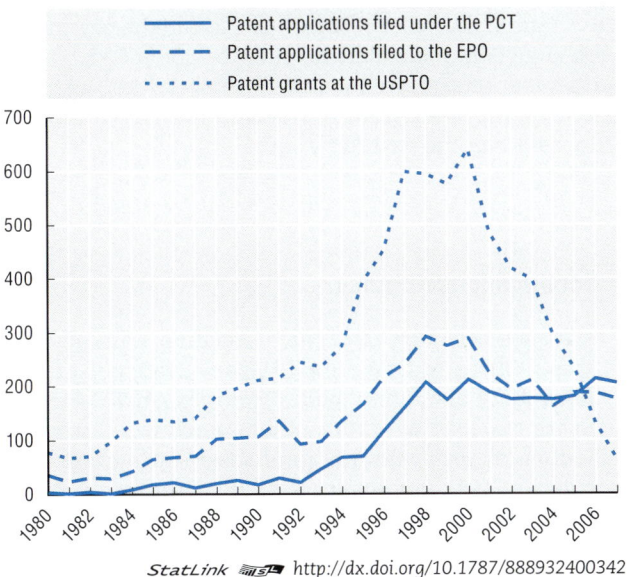

9.2 Breakdown of space-related patents by main domains (2000-08)
Number of patents by priority date (as a share of the total space-related patents over the period)

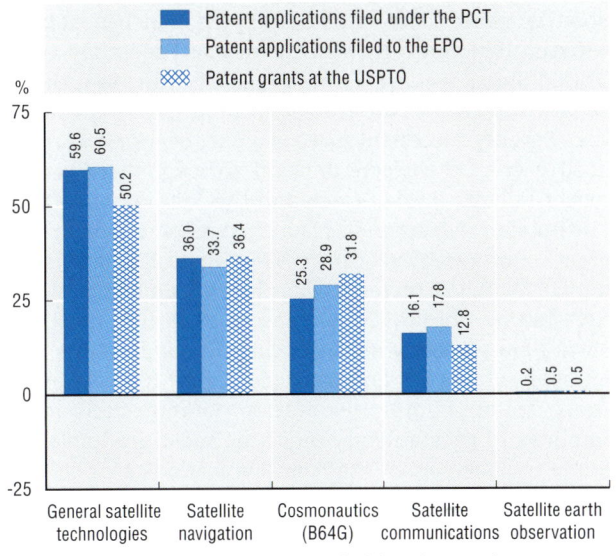

9.3 Country share in space-related patents (2000-08)
Patent applications filed under the Patent Co-operation Treaty by priority date and applicant's country

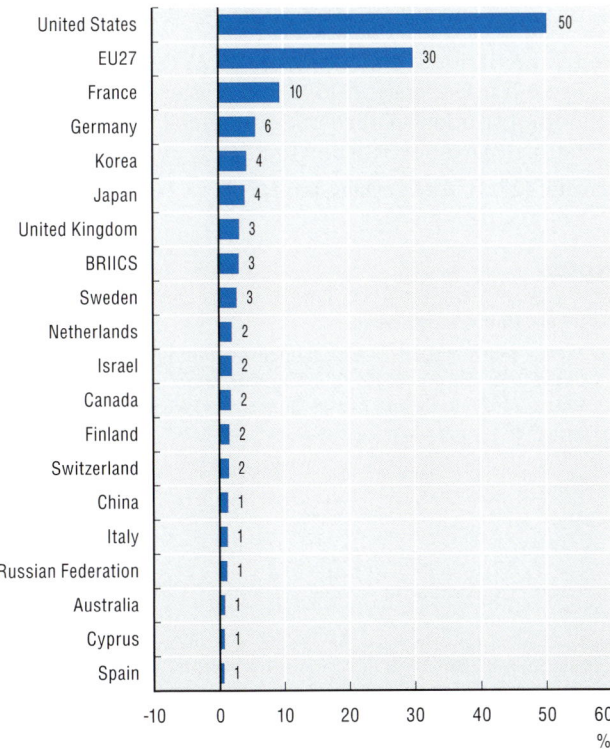

9.4 Revealed technological advantage in space related technologies
Patent applications filed under the Patent Co-operation Treaty by priority date and inventor's country

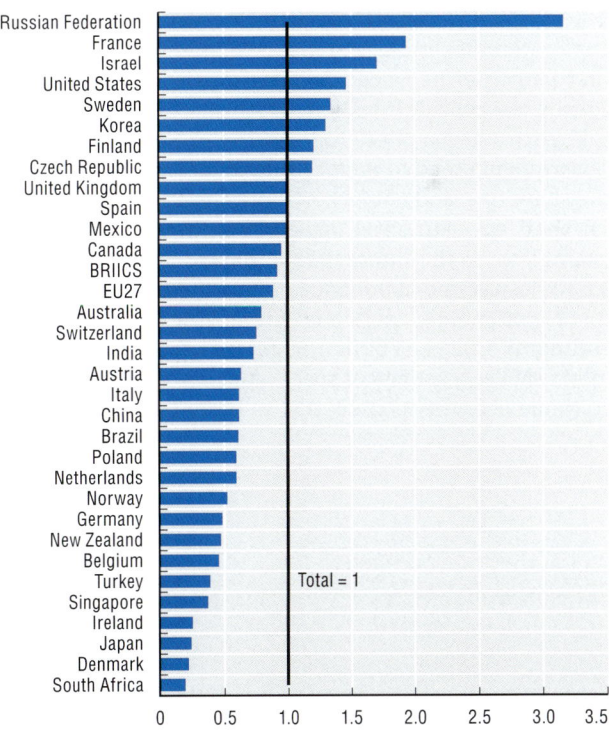

These figure is available online at: http://dx.doi.org/10.1787/888932400361.

III. INTENSITY: ACTIVITIES AND OUTPUTS IN THE SPACE ECONOMY

10. Space launch activities worldwide

Ten countries have so far demonstrated independent orbital launch capabilities, and seven countries (*i.e.* the United States, the Russian Federation, China, Japan, India, Israel and Iran) and the European Space Agency (ESA) have operational launchers. More than 1 100 space launches took place between 1994 and 2010, with the Russian Federation and the United States leading. From a high of 89 in 1994, the rate declined in 2001 to an average of around 60 launches per year. Seventy successful space launches occurred worldwide in 2010 with 119 payloads onboard, although there were four rocket failures (India, Korea and the Russian Federation). The Russian Federation has launched more rockets than any other country every year since 2006 (Figure 10.1) and is planning to launch 50 more satellites in 2011 alone. Countries in Asia led by China (15 launches in 2010, like the United States) are gradually outdistancing Europe in terms of the number of launches and payloads (Figure 10.2). As of 2011, there are six companies able to commercially launch satellites to geostationary orbit (the most profitable orbit, home to large commercial communications satellites): the European Arianespace company (the current market leader, with the Ariane 5 launcher), the Russian Federation's International Launch Services (Proton launcher), the United States' Lockheed Martin (Atlas V) and Boeing (Delta launchers), China Great Wall (Long March launchers) and Sea Launch, an international consortium (Norway, the Russian Federation, Ukraine and the United States) (Figure 10.3). Other companies can launch satellites in lower orbits (*e.g.* Orbital Sciences) or are planning to (*e.g.* Space Exploration Technologies). SpaceX conducted in 2010 the first launch of its Falcon 9, but also sent the commercial Dragon test capsule into orbit, which successfully re-entered the earth's atmosphere and landed in the Pacific Ocean. Governments tend to prefer using domestic launcher when they have one, and not rely on foreign commercial providers for their governmental payloads (military satellites, for examples). So the international market remains relatively small despite the abundance of launchers. Revenues from the 23 commercial launch events in 2010 amounted to an estimated USD 2.45 billion (Figure 10.4) (FAA, 2011). The relatively lively activity of space launches worldwide should continue over the next decade, as more governments fund earth observation, navigation, meteorological and other scientific and military satellites and develop new launchers. Already by the end of 2011, Europe could have three different rockets operating from its French Guiana spaceport (*i.e.* Ariane 5, the Russian Soyuz vehicle and the new smaller Vega launcher); India aims to enter the commercial market for geostationary satellites with a new rocket, and both Brazil and Korea aspire to develop their own national launchers over the next five years.

Methodological notes

Data are based on the Federal Aviation Administration's Office of Commercial Space Transportation (FAA/AST) and other public sources (*Air&Cosmos*, *Space News*). The data include worldwide orbital launch events that are conducted during a given calendar year, but not space shuttle launches, which carry astronauts (*i.e.* five space shuttle launches in 2010).

Sources

De Selding (2011), *Space News*, January.

Federal Aviation Administration (FAA) (2011), *Commercial Space Transportation: 2010 Year in Review*, Federal Aviation Administration's Office of Commercial Space Transportation (FAA/AST), Washington DC.

Lardier (2011), *Air&Cosmos*, January.

Notes

10.1: Asia: China, India, Japan.

10.2: One additional successful launch (including one payload) from Israel took place in 2010. Four launches were unsuccessful (1 from Korea, 2 from India and 1 from the Russian Federation).

III. INTENSITY: ACTIVITIES AND OUTPUTS IN THE SPACE ECONOMY

10. Space launch activities worldwide

10.1 Number of successful space launches (1994-2010)

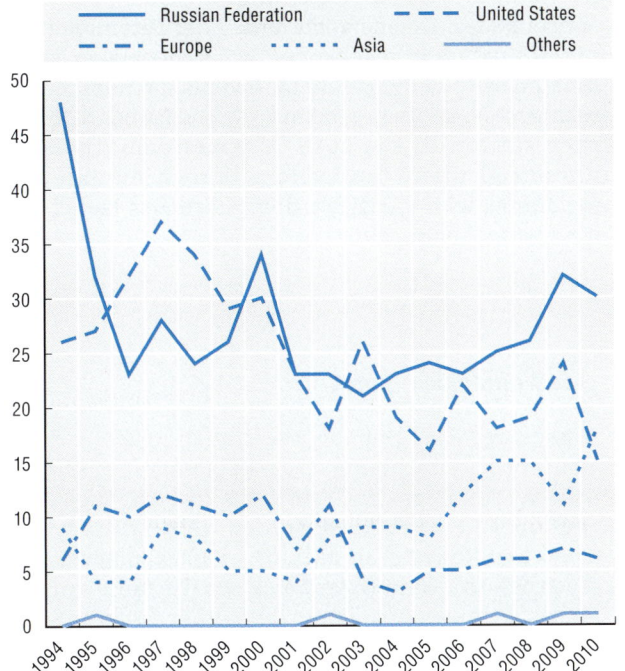

10.2 International distribution of successful space launches and payloads in 2010

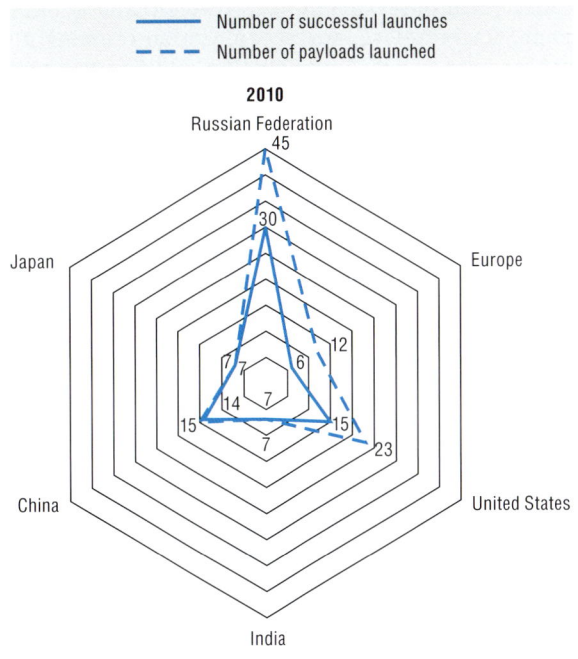

10.3 Commercial launch contracts signed in 2010

Number of contracts which may include one or more satellites to be launched over the coming years

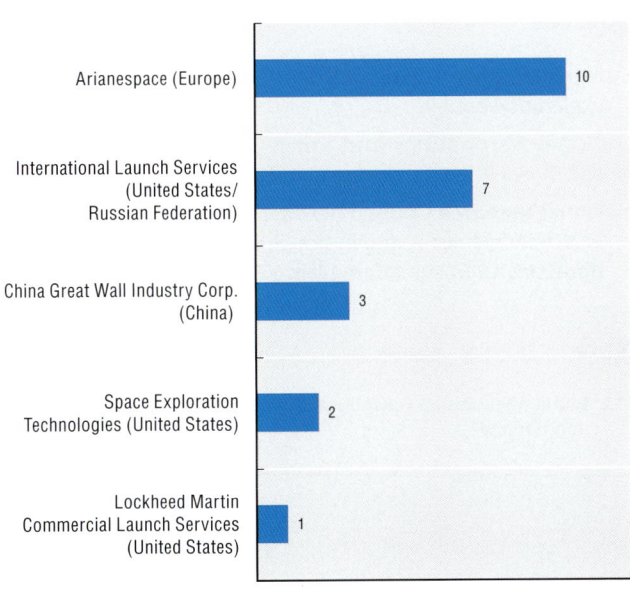

10.4 Launch industry revenues' estimates

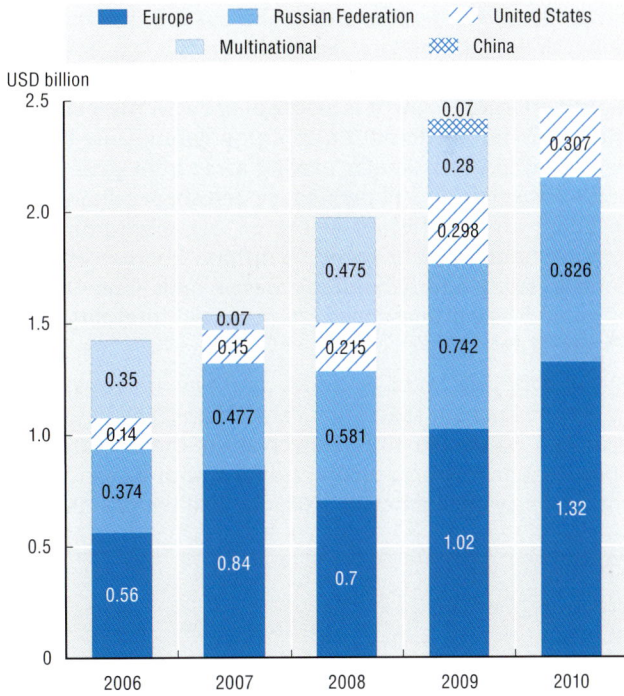

III. INTENSITY: ACTIVITIES AND OUTPUTS IN THE SPACE ECONOMY

11. Space exploration activities

Countries with space programmes are increasingly investing in down-to-earth space applications (*e.g.* telecommunications, earth observation) for strategic and economic reasons. Nevertheless, space exploration remains a key driver for investments in innovation and sciences, and it constitutes an intensive activity for major space agencies and industry. Significant achievements have attracted great public interest (*e.g.* landing on the Moon; Mars exploration by robots; probe landing on Titan).

Science and exploration. Space sciences and planetary missions have developed markedly over the years, with new actors joining in. This trend is reflected in the current and planned robotic exploration missions of the solar system, in which the United States, Europe, Japan, China and India are active players. As of the beginning of 2011, there are 3 satellites orbiting Mars (the United States, Europe), 2 active rovers on Mars' surface (the United States), 2 satellites orbiting Venus (the United States, China) and at least 7 probes flying throughout the solar system (Table 11.3). In 2009, Japan, India and China had all placed spacecraft into orbit around the Moon. In addition to those robotic missions targeted at extraterrestrial bodies, more than a dozen space science satellites are orbiting the earth. Two large international space telescopes (the United States, Europe) are active: the Hubble Space Telescope (launched in 1990, serviced in spring 2009) and SOHO, the Solar and Heliospheric Observatory (launched in 1995). Hubble's successor, the James Webb Space Telescope could be launched by NASA in 2014. Two other satellites are searching for earth-like planets outside the solar system: the international CoRoT observatory, led by the French Space Agency (launched in 2006) and NASA's Kepler observatory (launched in 2009). Swift is an ongoing NASA mission with international participation to study gamma-ray bursts (launched in 2004). Finally, moving away from earth orbit, ESA's Herschel and Planck space telescopes (launched in 2009) are positioned at the L2 Lagrange point – a gravitational stability point 1.5 million kilometres from earth to study infrared and microwave radiations. Dozens of ground-based telescopes are managed internationally (Figure 11.1).

Human spaceflight. More countries than ever are investing in indigenous human spaceflight capabilities (Table 11.2). The year 2011 marks the 13th anniversary of the International Space Station (ISS)'s on-orbit operations, with six astronauts continuously onboard since 2008, but also the planned end of the space shuttle programme. Over the past couple of years, a new generation of professional astronauts was selected in the United States, the European Space Agency member states, Canada and China. After becoming in 2008 the third nation to independently complete a spacewalk, China plans to demonstrate autonomous rendezvous and docking manoeuvres in orbit in 2011, and launch a 30-tonne space station in the 2016-22 timeframe. India also announced plans to develop its own human space programme, with a possible first indigenous launch of an Indian astronaut in 2016.

Methodological notes

Space agencies publish key statistics about their current and upcoming space exploration missions. Several definitions for "astronaut" co-exist. The International Aeronautic Federation (IAF) calls anyone who has flown at an altitude of 100 kilometres an "astronaut". The US Air Force set the limit at fifty miles altitude (80.45 km), while other organisations consider that a person must have reached orbital velocity and remain in orbit (above 200 km) to be considered an "astronaut". The IAF definition has been used in Table 11.2.

Sources

European Space Agency (2010), *Space Exploration*, http://exploration.esa.int.

National Aeronautics and Space Administration (NASA) (2010), *Solar System Exploration*, http://solarsystem.nasa.gov.

National Research Council (2010), *New Worlds, New Horizons in Astronomy and Astrophysics*, Space Studies Board, Aeronautics and Space Engineering Board, Washington DC.

Note

11.2: China, the Russian Federation, the United States. 7 Russian, 1 US, 1 international.

III. INTENSITY: ACTIVITIES AND OUTPUTS IN THE SPACE ECONOMY

11. Space exploration activities

11.1 Distribution of large optical infrared telescopes managed around the world

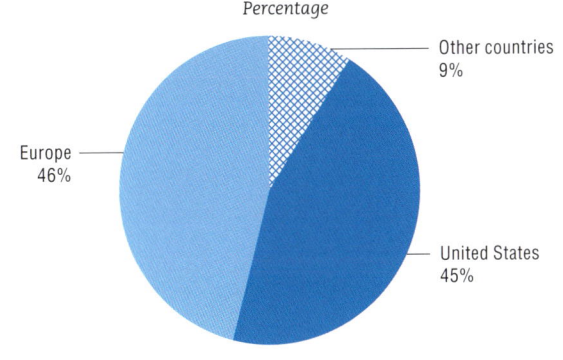

Percentage
- Europe 46%
- United States 45%
- Other countries 9%

11.2 Selected human spaceflight statistics
As of January 2011

Countries with autonomous capability to launch humans into space	3
Number of nationalities who have flown in space	40
Number of launches with humans onboard	+260
Persons who have flown into orbit	+510
Astronauts who walked on the Moon (1969-72)	12
Operational and inhabited space stations since the 1960s	9
Professional astronauts living in orbit (the International Space Station is continuously inhabited since 2003)	6
Number of paying orbital spaceflight participants ("space tourism")	7
Persons who have flown over the 100 km altitude threshold (including suborbital flights)	484

11.3 Planets and asteroids orbited and landed on since 1957
As of January 2011

Planet/celestial body	Number of missions	Number of planned missions	Orbiters	Landers/rovers	Selected missions
Mercury	2	2 (orbiters planned, ESA, Japan)	..	..	Messenger (flyby in 2008) to enter orbit in 2011 (NASA). BepiColombo to launch in 2013 (ESA, Japan).
Venus	+40	3 (NASA, ESA, the Russian Federation)	1 current orbiter (ESA Venus Express)	Last one: 1980 (the Russian Federation)	Venera 3 (the Russian Federation) was the first spacecraft to reach the surface of another planet in 1966.
Earth	+10 000 satellites launched since 1957	Hundreds	Almost a thousand operational satellites	..	Satellites used for communications, navigation, meteorology, climate and space science.
Earth's moon	+70	+10	2 current orbiters (NASA, China)	Latest one: 2010 (NASA)	Several orbiters and new rovers (China, India) are expected on the Moon by 2013-14.
Mars	+40	7 (NASA, the Russian Federation, Finland, China, ESA)	3 current orbiters (NASA, ESA)	2 current rovers (NASA)	Mariner 9 (1971, NASA, 1st successful orbit), Mars 3 (1971, the Russian Federation, 1st landing).
Phobos (Mars' moon)	..	1 (the Russian Federation, India)	..	..	Several flybys by probes on the way to Mars.
Jupiter	+5	2 (NASA)	Last one: 2003 (NASA)	..	Several flybys, making Jupiter the most visited of the Solar System's outer planets. Juno orbiter (NASA) should launch in 2011 and reach Jupiter by 2016.
Saturn	+5	..	1 current orbiter (NASA, ESA, Italy)	..	Several flybys by NASA probes since 1979 (Pioneer 11, Voyager 1 and 2).
Titan (Saturn's moon)	1	..	Last one: 2005 (NASA, ESA, Italy)	2005 (NASA, ESA, Italy)	The Huygens probe landed on Titan, Saturn's largest moon, in 2005.
Uranus	1	..	..	..	Flyby of the Voyager 2 probe (1986, NASA).
Neptune	1	..	..	..	Flyby of the Voyager 2 probe (1989, NASA).
Pluto (dwarf planet)	..	1 (NASA)	..	..	NASA's New Horizons space probe to fly by in 2015.
Asteroids and Comets	+15	2 (NASA, Japan)	Last one: 2010 (NASA)	Last one: 2005 (returned samples in 2010)	Japan landed on and brought back surface samples from the asteroid Itokawa (2010). ESA's Philae (on the Rosetta spacecraft) should land on Comet Churyumov-Gerasimenko in 2014. NASA's Dawn space probe to enter into Ceres' orbit in 2015 (dwarf planet).

IV. IMPACTS: BRINGING SPACE DOWN TO EARTH

12. Defining socio-economic impacts from space programmes

13. Indirect industrial effects

14. Economic growth (regional, national)

15. Efficiency/productivity gains

This chapter illustrates various types of socio-economic impacts derived from the development of space activities. The main message is that many space-based services have positive impacts on society, but issues concerning economic data definitions and methodologies have to be resolved to allow the benefits to be identified and quantified more precisely.

IV. IMPACTS: BRINGING SPACE DOWN TO EARTH

12. Defining socio-economic impacts from space programmes

The investments in space programmes are often justified by the scientific, technological, industrial and security capabilities they bring (Figure 12.1). The wish to develop a specialisation may allow a country to participate later on in large space programmes because of its expertise (*e.g.* Canada's expertise in robotics and radar imagery; Norway's expertise in developing satellite telecommunications in difficult environments, such as platforms at sea). Space investments can also provide socio-economic returns such as increased industrial activity, and bring cost efficiencies and productivity gains in other fields (*e.g.* weather forecasting, tele-medicine, environmental monitoring and agriculture previsions). Several space applications have reached technical maturity and have become the sources of new commercial downstream activities, sometimes far removed from the initial space research and development. For example, the growth of positioning, navigation and timing applications, which rely on satellite signals, has spurred new commercial markets (*e.g.* GPS chipsets in smartphones). But as Einstein wrote: "Not everything that counts, can be counted". This is also true for the diversity of socio-economic impacts derived from space activities. As shown in Figure 12.2, impacts can be categorised in different segments: new commercial products and services (including "indirect industrial effects" from space industry contracts, meaning new exports or new activities outside the space sector), productivity/efficiency gains in diverse economic sectors (*e.g.* fisheries, airlines), economic growth regionally and nationally, and cost avoidances (*e.g.* floods).The following sections review some of the impacts that have been detected so far.

Methodological notes

The most common economic measurement for any technology's value is the calculation of benefits to costs. In theory, to calculate the ratio, it is necessary to divide the benefits (*e.g.* improved productivity, decreased cost of operations, increased revenue and better customer satisfaction rates when applicable) by the costs of deploying the system (*e.g.* hardware, software, maintenance, training and so forth). However space systems are by nature multifaceted and rely often on lengthy research and development. The challenge of putting a monetary value on the technologies and services they deliver remains a complex and often subjective exercise. As discussed in OECD (2008), monetary or financial valuation methods fall into three basic types, each with its own repertoire of associated measurement issues and none of them entirely satisfactory on its own. They include: direct market valuation (*e.g.* market pricing), indirect market valuation (*e.g.* replacement cost) and survey-based valuation techniques (*i.e.* contingent valuation and group valuation). One option is to use several of these methods in parallel to test assumptions and the resulting impacts of a given space application. Ongoing work in OECD is devoted to conducting case studies on selected space applications, in order to provide a source of comparative national experiences and lessons learned when trying to apply the different methodologies to the study of impacts.

Source

OECD (2008), *Space Technologies and Climate Change*, OECD Publishing, Paris.

Further reading

OECD work on the space sector, *www.oecd.org/futures/space*.

OECD (2011), *Space Technologies and Food Security*, OECD Publishing, Paris (forthcoming).

IV. IMPACTS: BRINGING SPACE DOWN TO EARTH

12. Defining socio-economic impacts from space programmes

12.1 Examples of motivations for developing space programmes and possible developments over time

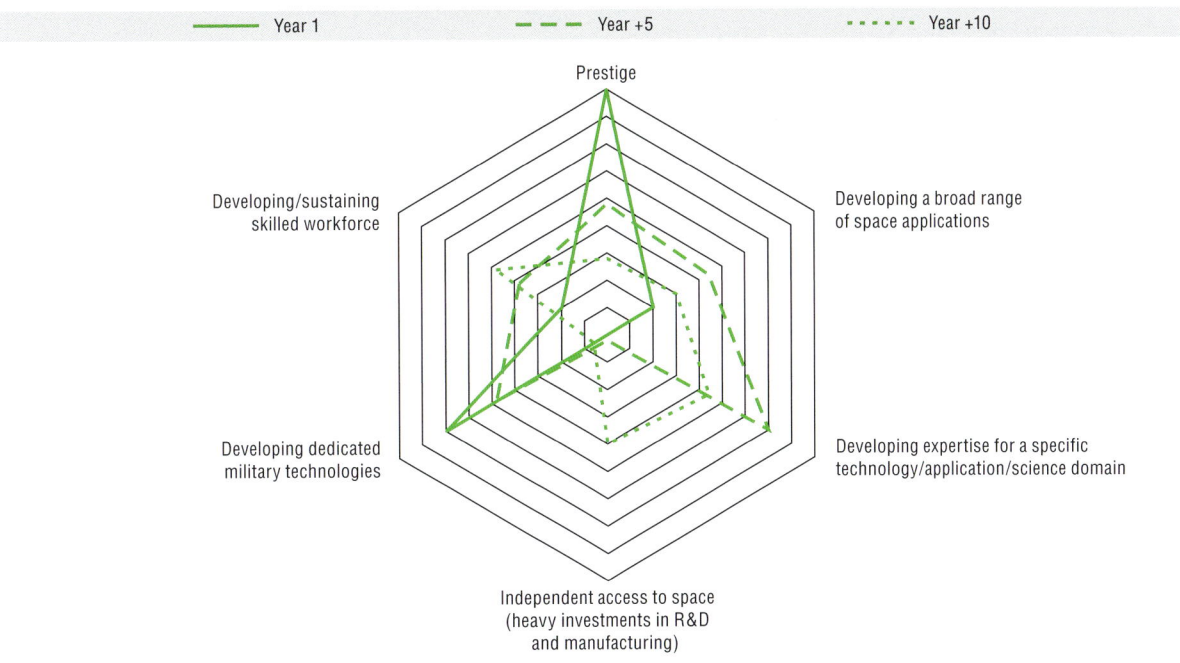

12.2 Review of possible impacts derived from investments in space programme

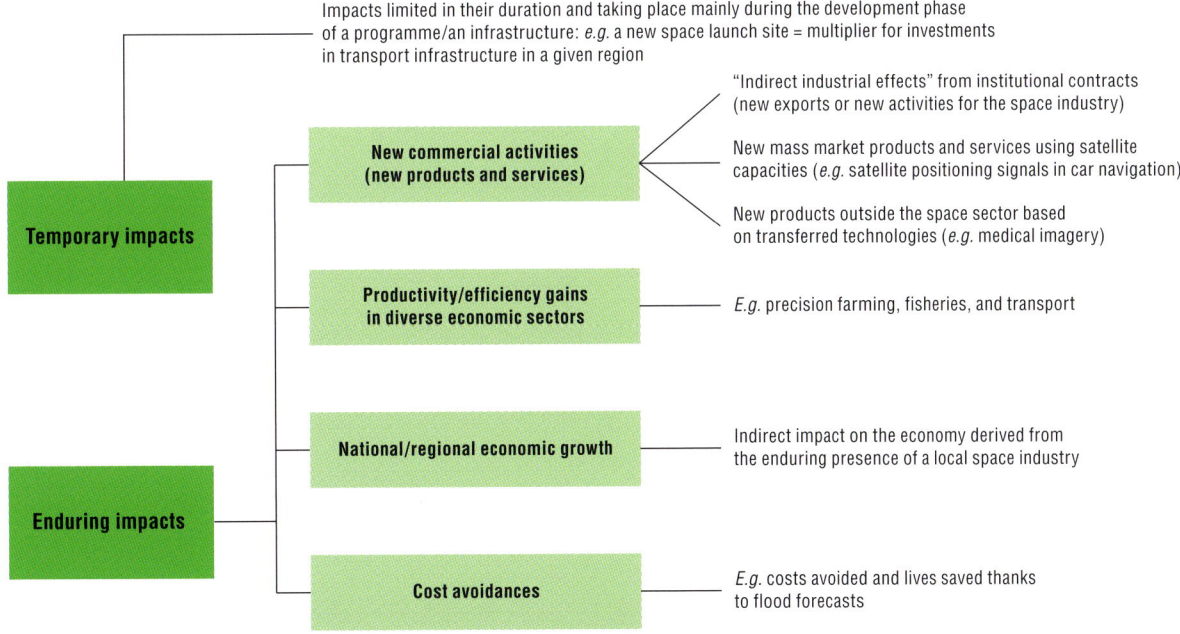

IV. IMPACTS: BRINGING SPACE DOWN TO EARTH

13. Indirect industrial effects

In a majority of countries, space programmes are contracted out to industry. The ability of firms to secure new customers or create new activities has been studied over the years, and although impacts may vary depending on the country and the level of its specialisation (*e.g.* applications *versus* manufacturing), there are several examples of positive industrial and economic returns from space investments, not only in countries with large space manufacturing industry but also in countries with smaller specialised space programmes.

- Norway – which has a small but active space programme – has detected a positive multiplier effect since the 1990s, *i.e.* in 2009, for each million Norwegian kroner of governmental support through the European Space Agency (ESA) or national support programmes, the Norwegian space sector companies have on average generated an additional turnover of NOK 4.7 million, usually as new exports or new activities outside the space sector (Norwegian Space Centre, 2010). This spin-off effect factor is expected to climb further as Norwegian space sector develops new products and services.
- In Belgium, the same type of multiplier has been detected (Capron, 2010). In 2010, for each EUR million of governmental support through ESA, it was found that EUR 1.4 million have been generated by the Belgian space industry.
- In Denmark, where some 25 companies are active in the space sector, each EUR million of Danish contributions to the European Space Agency has generated a turnover of EUR 3.7 million on average. Increased competencies within space activities through involvement in ESA projects is seen by the industry as facilitating the development of competencies in other sectors than the space sector (Danish Agency for Science, Technology and Innovation, 2008).

Methodological notes

The studies conducted by these countries have used different methodologies (*e.g.* input-outputs analysis, surveys). Already in the 1990s, the BETA (Bureau d'Économie Théorique et Appliquée) of the University Louis Pasteur had developed a methodology extensively applied to assess indirect economic effects of European Space Agency contracts in European member countries (BETA, 1989, 1997). Results showed already positive effects of ESA contracts for firms active in Europe and in Canada.

Sources

Capron, H., D. Baudewyns and M. Depelchin (2010), *Les établissements scientifiques fédéraux*, Collection Économie, Université Libre de Bruxelles (in French).

Danish Agency for Science, Technology and Innovation (2008), *Evaluation of Danish Industrial Activities in the European Space Agency (ESA): Assessment of the economic impacts of the Danish ESA-membership*, Copenhague, March.

Norwegian Space Centre (NSC) (2010), *Annual Report 2009*, March.

Further reading

OECD Main Science and Technology Indicators, www.oecd.org/sti/msti.

Notes

13.1: United Kingdom, United States: Economic growth multiplier (regional, national), not only indirect industrial effects.

IV. IMPACTS: BRINGING SPACE DOWN TO EARTH

13. Indirect industrial effects

13.1 Indirect industrial effects: multipliers in selected OECD countries
Multiplier calculated for 2009, or latest year

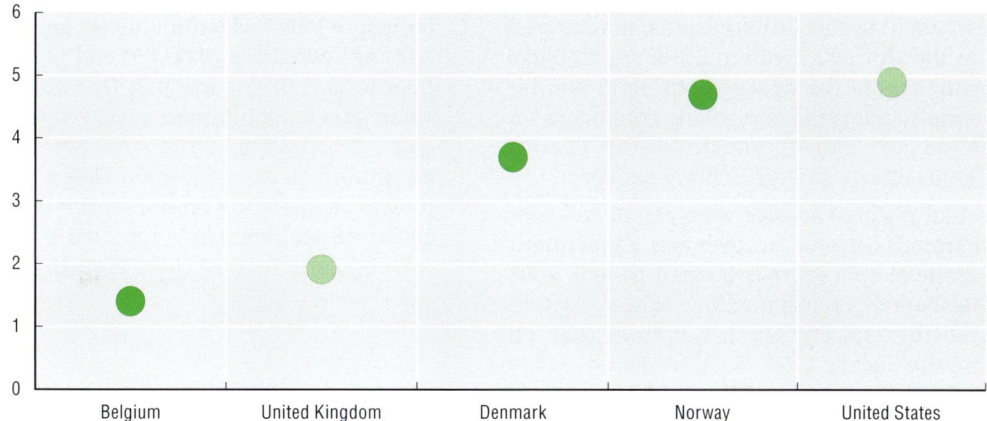

IV. IMPACTS: BRINGING SPACE DOWN TO EARTH

14. Economic growth (regional, national)

The macroeconomic impacts of space programmes at regional or even national levels have been measured in countries with significant space industry (manufacturing and/or services), such as the United States, France and most recently in the United Kingdom. Economic impacts analysis is not unique to the space sector, and similar studies on economic spillovers are regularly conducted for the automobile industry, the oil industry or the defence sector (*e.g.* economic effects of large military bases).

- In France, several regional studies were conducted over the years on French Guyana, an overseas department where the European spaceport is located (INSEE, 2008 and 2010). The share of value added due to space activities accounted for 21% of French Guyana's GDP on average during the decade 1965-75. With the advent of commercial launcher and Arianespace, the economic importance of space has risen sharply in the early 1990s (28.7% in 1991). It began to decline in 1994 (25.7%), and accelerated again in 2002-03 with new Ariane 5 launches. French Guyana exports predominantly consist of space transportation services sales by Arianespace. The ratio of exports to GDP is much higher than what is found in other French overseas territories. In 2009, space transportation services account for 90% of exports of French Guyana.
- In the United States, home of the biggest space industry in terms of employment and revenues, the most recent FAA study on the wider national economic impacts of the US commercial space activities has shown a rather stable multiplier ratio since 2002 (FAA, 2010). In 2009, for every dollar spent commercial space transportation industry, USD 4.9 resulted in indirect and induced economic impact. Using the same modeling techniques as the ones used for the aeronautic industry, the results show that many economic sectors may be impacted by commercial space activities, as they provide goods and services, directly or indirectly, to the space industry. In 2009, the Information Services industry was the most affected group in terms of additional economic activity, earnings and jobs, generating over USD 65.4 billion of revenue, over USD 15.3 billion in earnings, and creating 213 230 jobs (Table 14.1).
- In the United Kingdom, where the downstream space services' sector have been growing steadily (boosted by the satellite communications sector), a national economic impacts study was also conducted recently. Including both upstream and downstream actors (from satellite manufacturers to operators and providers of services), the space industry's value-added multiplier on the British economy has been estimated to be 1.91 and the employment multiplier to be 3.34 (Figure 14.2). The space industry's direct value-added contribution to GDP was estimated at some GBP 3.8 billion and the indirect economic impacts amounted to an additional GBP 3.3 billion (*i.e.* space industry's spending on non-space UK inputs). The total UK-based employment supported by the space industry was estimated to be 83 000 in 2009 (UK Space Agency, 2010).

Methodological notes

The American and French economic impact studies apply different input/output methods, while the United Kingdom analysis is based on the results of industry survey responses. The FAA uses the Regional Input-Output Modelling System (RIMS II) developed by the Department of Commerce, Bureau of Economic Analysis. The French national statistical office INSEE has used different impacts methodologies over time.

Sources

Federal Aviation Administration (FAA) (2010), *The Economic Impact of Commercial Space Transportation on the US Economy in 2009*, Federal Aviation Administration's Office of Commercial Space Transportation, Washington DC, September.

Institut National de la Statistique et des Études Économiques (INSEE) (2008), *Impact du spatial sur l'économie de la Guyane*, September (in French).

INSEE (2010), *Les comptes économiques de la Guyane en 2009 : Le spatial préserve la croissance*, September (in French).

UK Space Agency (UKSA) (2010), *The size and health of the UK space industry*, Swindon, Wiltshire, November.

IV. IMPACTS: BRINGING SPACE DOWN TO EARTH

14. Economic growth (regional, national)

14.1 Distribution of economic activity, earnings and jobs throughout major US industry groups, generated by commercial space transportation in 2009

Industry	Annual economic activity (USD thousands)	Annual earnings (USD thousands)	Jobs (actual)
Information	65 439 541	15 300 588	213 230
Manufacturing	55 057 996	10 344 418	139 330
Real estate and rental and leasing	14 117 305	1 045 577	26 460
Finance and insurance	10 293 180	2 837 099	41 270
Wholesale trade	9 604 696	3 086 597	49 520
Professional, scientific and technical services	8 924 227	3 907 575	67 580
Health care and social assistance	7 573 426	3 686 542	86 910
Retail trade	6 433 283	2 186 157	83 970
Transportation and warehousing	4 953 733	1 721 070	37 490
Other services	4 488 631	1 487 338	49 580
Accommodation and food services	3 838 417	1 468 241	78 590
Management of companies	3 642 211	1 798 479	19 860
Administrative and waste management services	3 433 803	1 444 426	53 400
Arts, entertainment and recreation	2 943 346	1 134 515	39 430
Utilities	2 770 861	513 427	4 950
Agriculture, forestry, fishing and hunting	1 906 597	279 481	11 170
Educational Services	1 209 871	548 406	18 630
Mining	976 568	191 344	2 130
Construction	721 322	276 068	5 960
Total	**208 329 012**	**53 257 346**	**1 029 460**

Source: FAA (2010).

14.2 Economic impact of the UK space industry, 2008-09
Contribution to GDP in GBP million and jobs

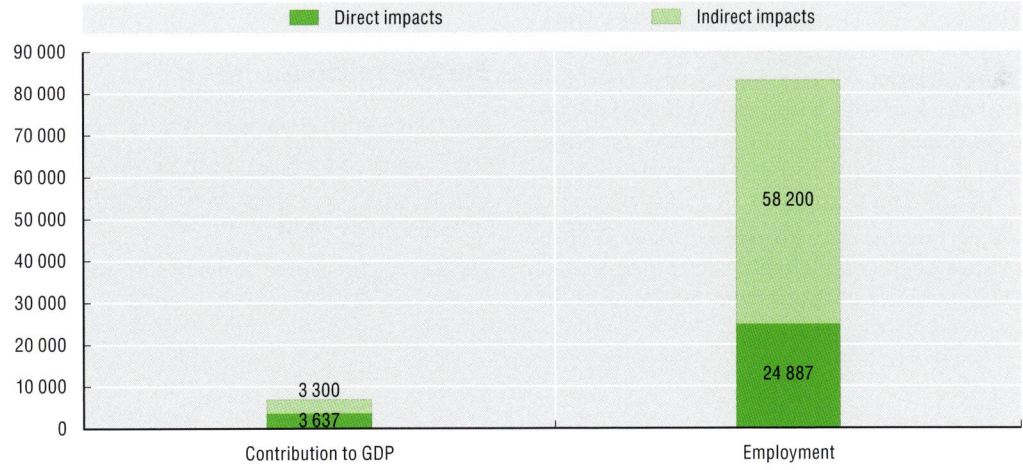

Source: UKSA (2010).

IV. IMPACTS: BRINGING SPACE DOWN TO EARTH

15. Efficiency/productivity gains

The amount of efficiency and productivity gains derived from the use of space applications across very diverse sectors of the economy keeps growing over the years. From agriculture to energy, institutional actors and private companies are using satellite signals and imagery with positive returns as demonstrated in examples and box "How satellites are changing agricultural practices and contributing to food security". Satellites can also play a key role in providing communications infrastructure rapidly to areas lacking any ground infrastructure, contributing to link rural and isolated areas with urbanised centres (Table 15.1).

- *Positioning and navigation efficiencies*. Adoption of satellite navigation-related technologies in fishing fleets began in the mid-1980s, and general technology rollout and adoption began in the mid-1990s all over the world. Based on efficiency gains studies, the fishing power of the commercial Australian fleet increased since the uptake of GPS and plotters. The cumulative addition to fishing output that were conservatively attributed to the use of GPS plotters was estimated at 4.14% of output in 2007, equivalent to around AUD 88 million at 2007 prices (OECD, 2008).
- *Higher perspectives from space*. The specific topographic perspectives brought by earth observation and navigation satellites allow cost-efficiencies. In India, a large petrochemical group uses remote sensing to plan several pipeline routings for the transportation and distribution of natural gas/hydrocarbons. Building a geographic information system with imagery from the Indian Cartosat-1 satellite and cadastral data, the company's field work time was reduced from 90% to less than 15% from previous conventional surveys (usually only 1.5 to 2 km were covered per day compared with more than a hundred of kilometres with satellites). Updates in the imagery database will help monitor the pipeline routing areas and create long-term time series (ISRO, 2010).
- *Technology transfers from the space programme*. Many studies of "spin-offs" have been conducted in the United States since the 1960s (such as outputs from NASA's Apollo programme), focusing on the transfers from space-related hardware and know-how to other sectors (NASA, 2010). There are more than 1 600 NASA-derived technologies that have been transferred to other sectors, bringing efficiency gains particularly in medical imagery (*e.g.* Hubble telescope's optics used for increased precision in micro-invasive arthroscopic surgery).

Methodological notes

In the case of space applications, the study of productivity gains are often conducted as *ad hoc* reports, therefore methodologies may vary and render difficult international comparability. The OECD is building up a database of existing indicators, as to provide access to data and methodological information.

Sources

Indian Space Research Organisation (ISRO) (2010), *www.isro.org*.

National Aeronautics and Space Administration (NASA) (2010), *US Space Programme Spin-off*, www.sti.nasa.gov/tto.

OECD (2008), *Space Technologies and Climate Change*, OECD Publishing, Paris.

Further reading

OECD Productivity Database, www.oecd.org/statistics/productivity.

OECD Work on the Space Sector, www.oecd.org/futures/space.

OECD (2011a), *OECD-FAO Agricultural Outlook*, OECD Publishing, Paris.

OECD (2011b), *Space Technologies and Food Security*, OECD Publishing, Paris (forthcoming).

IV. IMPACTS: BRINGING SPACE DOWN TO EARTH

15. Efficiency/productivity gains

How satellites are changing agricultural practices and contributing to food security

As many countries seek to ensure self-sufficiency in production of selected commodities, satellite data often represent a good option to complement or even replace ground monitoring systems, which are not easily deployable or too expensive to set up.

- *Near real time products.* Users, whether policy-makers, farmers or researchers, can find today a range of near real time products providing information on vegetation and land use, particularly on what types of crops are being planted nationally and around the world (*e.g.* 3 hour latency for NASA-MODIS products on soil moisture for example).

- *Improved cadastral information.* In many countries there is a growing need for governments and farmers to better map their arable land. In India, the Ministry of Rural Development is leading the "National Land Records Modernization Programme", which aims to check private cadastral information and improve land-use planning nationally. It relies on data from the dozen or so Indian remote sensing satellites. In Europe, the Common Agriculture Policy provides direct aid to farmers, with amounts distributed in part per declared square metre of land. European Commission inspectors are using commercial precision farming products, positioning and remote sensing data, to check whether the area declared by farmers is eligible.

- *Increasing cost efficiencies.* Although precision agriculture remains a niche market, many farmers in several OECD countries (*e.g.* Canada, France, the United States) have started using devices with GPS signals and satellite imagery for the entire agriculture cycle: planning (surveying their fields and crop varieties); planting (making sure the planting is done on straight lines); crop protection (spaying insecticides, fertilisers per square metre) and harvesting (helping enhance crop yields by making sure farming machines follow straight lines). Reduction of fertilisers and pesticides is one of the key benefits of using precision agriculture.

- *Better irrigation practices.* Adequate irrigation is essential to improve food productivity in many regions, especially as fresh water is becoming scarcer. In India, under the "Rajiv Gandhi National Drinking Water Mission" of Ministry of Rural Development, remote sensing technology is already used for preparing groundwater maps in ten states. The success rate of bore wells is already around 90% in most States. The project is now being extended in phases to cover the entire country.

15.1 Space applications providing unique societal services

	Key facts	Space applications bringing societal services
Indonesia	Inhabitants: 271.4 million. The territory constitutes of 17 000 islands in three time zones.	Tele-education: the Indonesian palapa satellite system provides tele-education programmes via television broadcasts. With the launch of the latest Palapa satellite, the 2011 target is to provide increased access for approximately 43 000 rural villages.
India	Inhabitants: 1.144 million, nearly 700 million live in 600 000 villages.	• Tele-education: The dedicated Indian Edusat satellite permits to reach 55 000 virtual classrooms, allowing two-way communications in many cases. • Telemedecine: the Indian fleet of telecommunications satellites, the Insat network, connected already 382 medical facilities in June 2010 (306 district/rural hospitals, 60 specialty hospitals, 16 mobile units).
Thailand	Inhabitants: 67.7 million.	Tele-education: Thai education programmes are transmitted via the second generation Thaicom satellite systems to some 3 000 secondary schools and 7 000 primary schools in Thailand.

V. NATIONAL SPOTLIGHTS ON SELECTED COUNTRIES

16. United States

17. France

18. Italy

19. Canada

20. United Kingdom

21. Norway

22. India

23. China

24. Brazil

This chapter presents space developments in selected space-faring countries, particularly members of the OECD Forum on Space Economics. The countries covered are the United States, France, Italy, Canada, the United Kingdom, Norway, India, China and Brazil. The data come from official sources (such as national space agencies, statistical offices, OECD databases), as well as private sources in some cases. Figures have been chosen based on the reliability and the timeliness of available data.

V. NATIONAL SPOTLIGHTS ON SELECTED COUNTRIES

16. United States

The United States has the largest space programme in the world, involving several civilian and defence-related organisations. In addition to the National Aeronautics and Space Administration (NASA), other public organisations have dedicated -although often not well identified – space budgets: the Department of Defense, the Department of Energy, the Department of Transportation (Office of Commercial Space Transportation), the Department of Commerce's National Oceanic and Atmospheric Administration and the US Geological Survey. The overall budget is estimated conservatively at approximately USD 48.8 billion in 2010. NASA has a budget totaling USD 18.72 billion in 2010, up from USD 17.78 billion in 2009 (Figure 16.2). NASA has 16 centers and facilities located throughout the United States. About two-thirds of NASA's budget is associated with human spaceflight while the rest is distributed between science missions (earth science, planetary science, heliophysics and astrophysics) and aeronautics. Although the outlays for NASA have increased overall since the early 2000s, NASA's share has largely declined then stagnated since the Apollo programme when compared to the total outlays of US agencies. It represents 0.5% of the US budget (Figure 16.3). Industry-wise, the US space sector relies on a large aerospace and defense manufacturing base. American aerospace manufacturers employed some 503 900 workers in 2009 in 3 100 establishments, not including aerospace R&D-related workers employed in other establishments (Table 16.1). The largest numbers of aerospace jobs are located in California and Washington, although many are also located in Texas, Kansas, Connecticut and Arizona (US Department of Labor, 2010).

Methodological notes

The official US statistics on manufacturing come from the US Census Bureau's Annual Survey of Manufactures and encompass three industry groupings from the North American Industrial Classification System (NAICS): 336414 (Guided missiles and space vehicle manufacturing), 336415 (Guided missiles and space propulsion unit and propulsion unit parts manufacturing) and 336419 (Other guided missile and space vehicle parts and auxiliary equipment manufacturing). As it is not possible to separate the missiles from space vehicles, the two are together termed the US "space industry".

Sources

National Aeronautics and Space Administration (NASA) (2010), *Fiscal Year 2011 Budget Estimate*, NASA, Washington DC.

The White House (2010), *The White House Office of Management and Budget*, Washington DC, www.whitehouse.gov/omb.

US Census Bureau (2010), *2009 Annual Survey of Manufactures*, Statistics for Industry Groups and Industries, 12 March, Washington DC.

US Department of Labor (2010), *Career Guide to Industries: Aerospace Product and Parts Manufacturing*, Washington DC, Bureau of Labor Statistics, www.bls.gov/oco/cg/.

V. NATIONAL SPOTLIGHTS ON SELECTED COUNTRIES

16. United States

16.1 The US aerospace and space industry in 2009
Number of employees, value of shipments and value added

	Aerospace product and parts manufacturing	Guided missile and space vehicle manufacturing	Space vehicle propulsion unit and parts manufacturing	Other guided missile and space vehicle parts manufacturing
Number of employees	429 777	50 338	15 486	7 662
Average wage per hour (USD)	33.63	33.87	31	25
Total value of shipments (USD 1 000)	178 924 241	16 141 661	4 521 328	1 227 563
Value added (USD 1 000)	99 173 054	9 646 809	3 076 885	750 847
NAICS code	3 364	336 414	336 415	336 419

Source: US Census Bureau (2010) and US Department of Labor (2010).

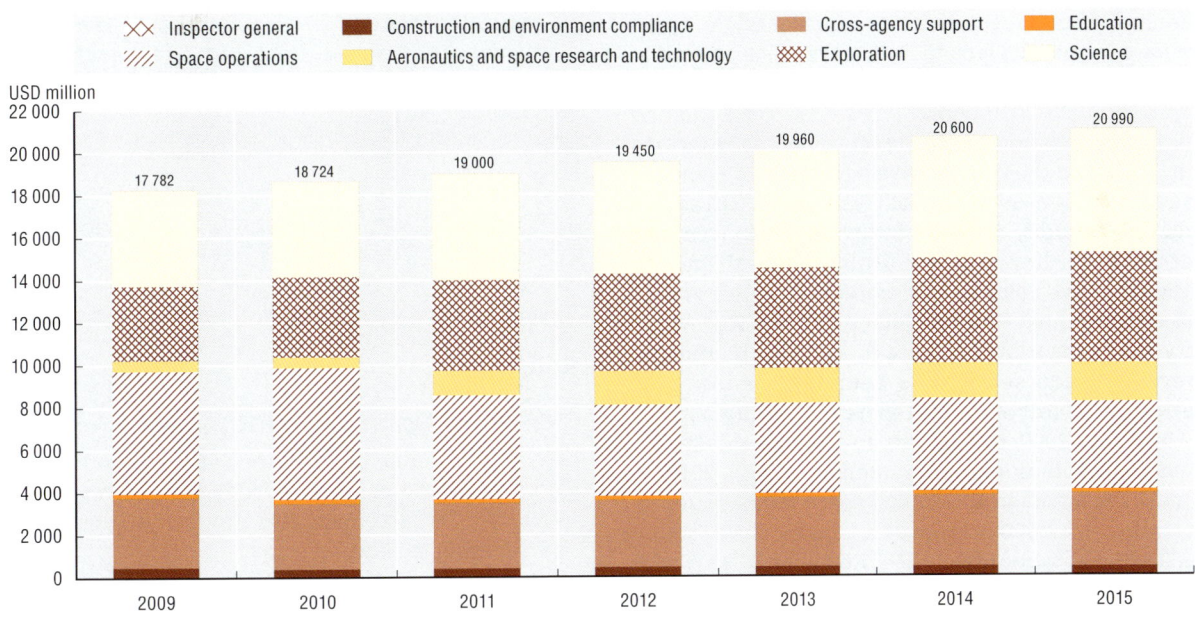

16.2 Estimates for NASA funding for 2010-15

Source: NASA (2010).

StatLink http://dx.doi.org/10.1787/888932400437

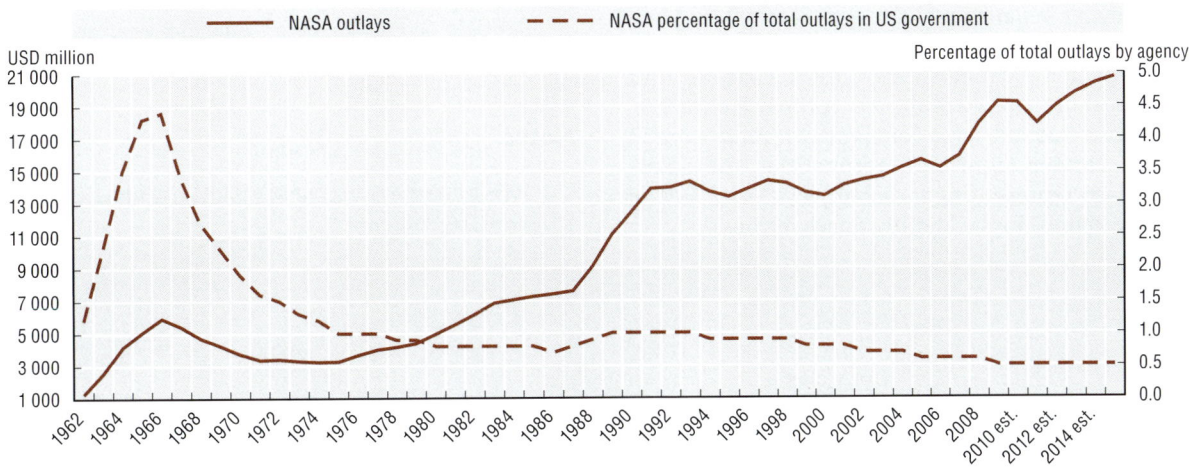

16.3 NASA outlays and NASA's percentage of US governmental agencies' total outlays, 1962-2015

Source: The White House (2010).

StatLink http://dx.doi.org/10.1787/888932400456

V. NATIONAL SPOTLIGHTS ON SELECTED COUNTRIES

17. France

Placed under the joint supervision of the Ministry of Higher Education and Research and the Department of Defense, the French space agency (Centre national d'études spatiales – CNES) had a budget of EUR 1.97 billion in 2010 (of which EUR 685 million earmarked for the European Space Agency). France is the first financial contributor to the European Space Agency, followed by Germany and Italy. The 2010-15 accord signed in late 2010 by the French government and the French space agency provides for an additional EUR 15 million grant to CNES national programme (called "multilateral", because it often involves international partners). In 2011, CNES also manages EUR 500 million in French public bonds in order to stimulate research and future economic growth, via investments in the next generation of European launcher and innovative satellites. The aerospace sector represents an important source of economic growth for the French economy, as shown by the trend in air freight and space transport revenues over the 1995-2010 period (Figure 17.2). Aeronautic and space specialisation in the French economy remained strong in 2010, and the comparative advantage of France in this area has risen over the last ten years (Direction générale des douanes et droits indirects, 2010) (see also Chapter VI). According to the *OECD International Trade by Commodity Statistics Database*, the trade balance for French aerospace represented USD 18.3 billion in 2009. The overall industry has shown strong growth since 2005 and the commercial space sector has seen expansion over the period with unconsolidated revenues up 22% to EUR 3.9 billion in 2009, due in part to a strong market for commercial telecommunications satellites (GIFAS, 2010). A focus on 27 key actors in the French space industry, representing almost 12 000 employees, shows that French consolidated sales amounted to EUR 2.6 billion in 2009 with 35% of revenues coming from commercial exports (Figure 17.3) (Eurospace, 2010). In addition to French Guyana, which hosts the European spaceport, France has three major regional aerospace clusters: the *Aerospace Valley* in the Aquitaine and Midi-Pyrénées regions, with Toulouse representing the first aerospace pole in Europe, with more than 220 French and international companies; the *ASTech* cluster in Paris and its region, representing half of the French R&D aerospace employment; and finally the *Pégase* cluster in Provence-Alpes-Côte-d'Azur, around Cannes with more than a hundred companies (INSEE, 2010a). In those clusters, large companies' revenues are in many cases derived from both aeronautics and space activities, space representing for example 7.3% to 13% of companies' revenues in the Midi-Pyrénées region.

Methodological notes

The national statistical office INSEE conducts regional surveys in Midi-Pyrénées (annual since 1982), Aquitaine (annual since 2000) and French Guyana (regular, not annual) specifically on manufacturers, subcontractors, and service providers in the aeronautical and space sectors. These surveys provide snapshots of the French aerospace industry, an important sector for the economies of those three French regions in terms of revenue and employment. Since 1st January 2008, a new French classification system is used (*Nomenclature d'activités française* – NAF Rev. 2) and the two regions Midi-Pyrénées and Aquitaine benefit from a common survey, which allows even more detailed comparable data. Eurospace conducts annual surveys on the European space industry.

Sources

CNES (2010), *Rapport d'activité 2009*, Paris.

Direction générale des douanes et droits indirects (2010), "Le chiffre du commerce extérieur", *Études et éclairages*, No. 15, Département des statistiques et des études économiques, July.

Eurospace (2010), *The European Space Industry in 2009, Facts and Figures*, 14th Edition, Paris, August.

Groupement des industries Françaises Aéronautiques et Spatiales (GIFAS) (2010), *Annual Report 2008-2009*, GIFAS, Paris, July.

Institut National de la Statistique et des Études Économiques (INSEE) (2010), "Début 2010, l'aéronautique encore au ralenti, le spatial accélère", *Aquitaine e-publications*, INSEE, Paris, July.

Notes

17.1: 2009 includes working capital of EUR 16 million.
17.2: Up to May 2010 only.

V. NATIONAL SPOTLIGHTS ON SELECTED COUNTRIES

17. France

17.1 CNES budget 2008-09
Current EUR million

	2008	2009
Revenues		
Government subsidies	1 376	1 424
External contracts	355	553
Total revenues	1 731	1 977
Expenditures		
France's contribution to ESA	685	685
Multilateral programme	1 042	1 292
Access to space (launchers)	361	396
Utilisation of space	566	776
Pooled resources	116	122
Civil applications	36	43
Earth, environment, climate	87	87
Space sciences, preparing the future	171	170
Security and defence	156	354
Central directorates	53	49
VAT and payroll taxes	62	71
Total expenditures	1 727	1 977

Source: CNES (2010).

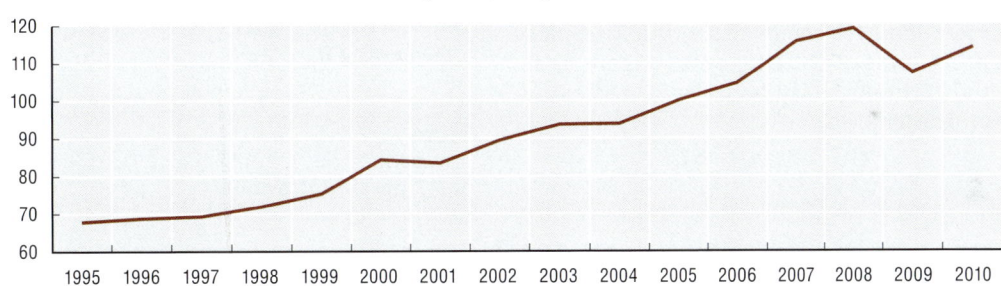

17.2 Revenues in air freight and space transport, 1995-2010
Annual average index, base year 2005 = 100

Source: Direction générale des douanes et droits indirects (2010).

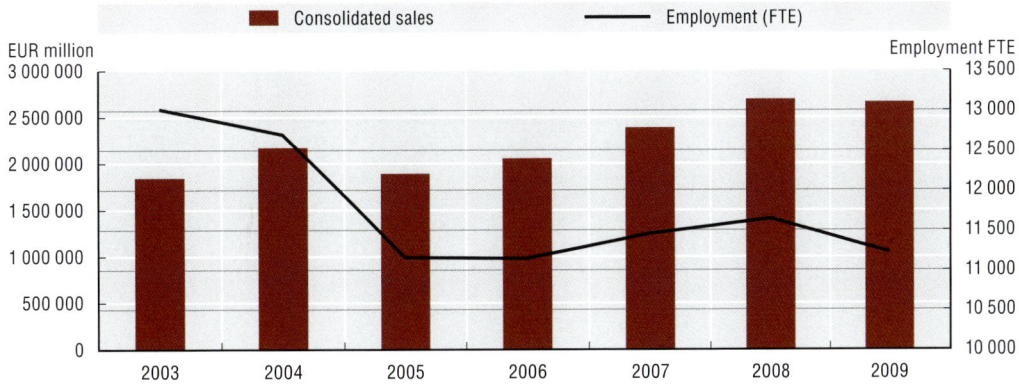

17.3 Employment and consolidated sales in French space sector, 2003-09
Sales in current EUR million and employment in FTE

Source: Eurospace (2010).

THE SPACE ECONOMY AT A GLANCE 2011 © OECD 2011

V. NATIONAL SPOTLIGHTS ON SELECTED COUNTRIES

18. Italy

The Italian space agency, *Agenzia Spaziale Italiana* (ASI), is headquartered in Rome with three centers in Matera, Trapani Malindi (Kenya), and the ASI Science Data Center (ASDC) in *Frascati*, near Rome. Italy is the third-largest contributor to the European Space Agency (after France and Germany), and is actively involved in all domains of space applications and space exploration. The Italian Space Agency budget is around EUR 700 million a year. The ten-year strategic plan (2010-20) earmarks EUR 7.2 billion in funding over the period, and should provide approximately the same level of spending annually. The main funding ministries include mainly the Ministry for Instruction, Universities and Research, which allocates EUR 600 million per year and the Ministry of Defence for dual missions such as COSMO-SkyMed and Athena-Fidus. In terms of expenditures, as shown in Figure 18.1, Italy's contribution to ESA represents the first budget line over the next decade, although the strategic plan aims to slightly rebalance expenditures in favour of the national programme and bilateral co-operation, reducing the Italian annual payment to ESA from EUR 400 million to around EUR 385 million (ASI, 2010).

Programme-wise, earth observation remains a priority with more than one-third of the overall budget allocated (Figure 18.2). Deep space missions and access to space technologies represent respectively 25% and 19% of the overall budget. Italy also aims to re-enter the satellite telecommunications sector, particularly via the development of public-private partnerships with commercial companies. Italy has more than 180 companies in the aerospace sector, representing some 35 000 employees (Figure 18.3). Besides the dual systems, Italy has also a dedicated military space programme.

Methodological notes

The budget data come from the Italian space agency's strategic plan (released in December 2010). The data for the aerospace industry's turnover and production have been calculated using monthly data from the Italian national statistics office *ConIstat Database*, while the number of aerospace companies and employees in Italy are based on data from the Istat Database. The industry classification used is "Manufacture of air and spacecraft and related machinery" (Nace 2.2), which may not cover all actors in the Italian aerospace and defense industry.

Sources

Association of Italian Industries for Aerospace Systems and Defence (Associazione Industrie per l'Aerospazio i sistemi e la Difesa) (AIAD), *www.aiad.it*.

Association for Space-based Applications and Services (Associazione per I Servizi, le Applicazioni e le Tecnologie ICT per lo Spazio) (ASAS), *www.asaspazio.it*.

Italian Space Agency (ASI) (2010), *Strategic Plan 2010-2020*, Italian Space Agency, Rome, December.

National Italian Institute of Statistics (Istat) Database (2010), *www.istat.it*.

Note

18.4: Figures up to May 2010.

V. NATIONAL SPOTLIGHTS ON SELECTED COUNTRIES

18. Italy

18.1 Planned distribution of Italian space budget in the 2010-20 period
Percentage

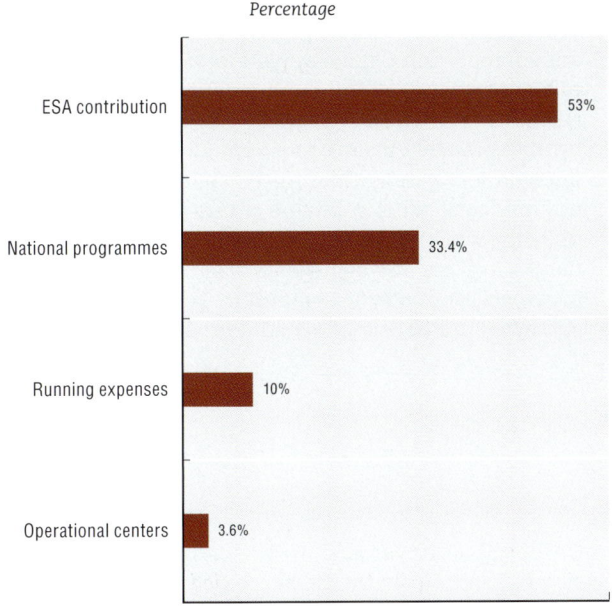

Source: ASI (2010).

18.2 Planned Italian space programme's expenditures by sector in the 2010-20 period
Percentage

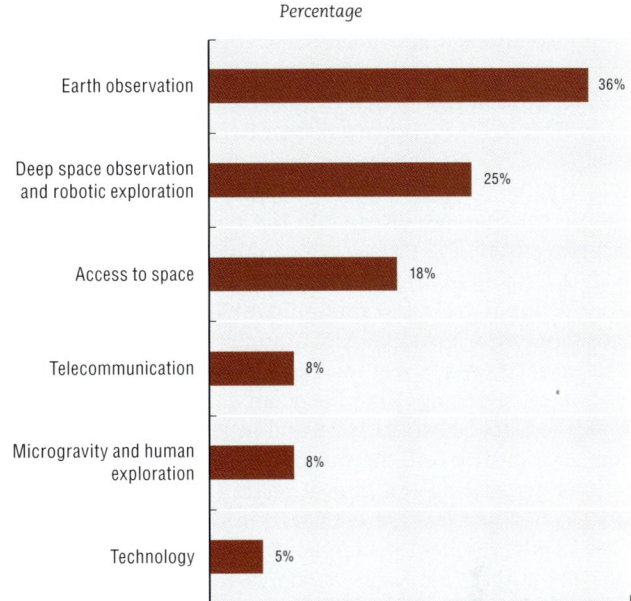

Source: ASI (2010).

18.3 Number of aerospace companies and employees in Italy

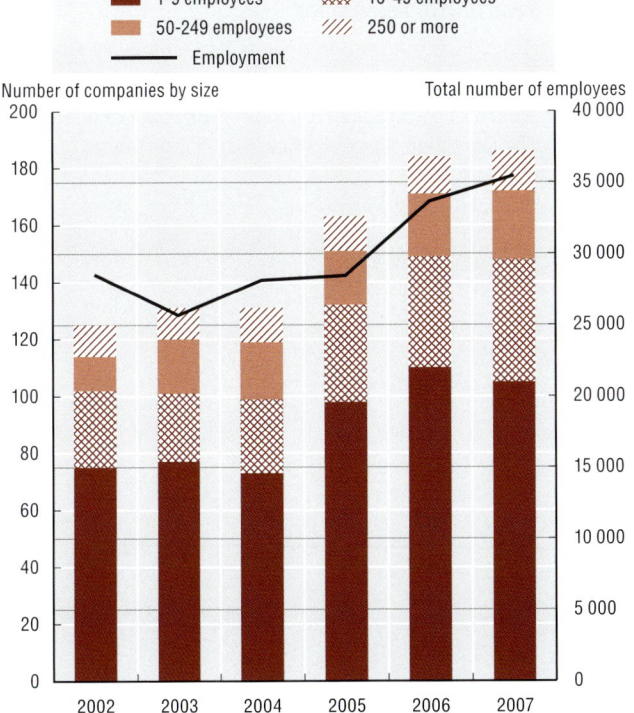

Source: OECD calculations based on ISTAT (2010).

18.4 Production and turnover in the Italian aerospace industry
ISIC category: "Manufacture of air and spacecraft and related machinery"

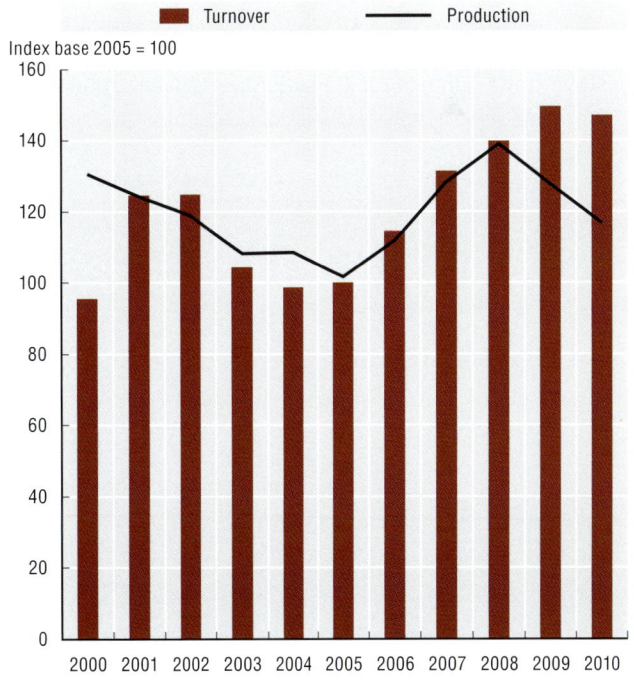

Source: OECD calculations based on ISTAT (2010).

THE SPACE ECONOMY AT A GLANCE 2011 © OECD 2011

V. NATIONAL SPOTLIGHTS ON SELECTED COUNTRIES

19. Canada

Canada has developed over the years a dynamic space programme, positioning its space industry with comparative advantages in several niche areas, including robotics, satellite communications and satellite radar imagery. The Canadian Space Agency (CSA) had a budget of some CAD 344 million in 2009-10 fiscal year, which could decrease over the next four years (Figure 19.1). However, the CSA received in 2010 an additional CAD 397 million over five years to develop, with the industry, the next generation of Canadian advanced radar remote sensing satellites, with the bulk of this spending occurring after 2011 (Treasury Board of Canada, 2010). And in 2009, Canada's *Economic Action Plan* provided the CSA with an additional CAD 110 million over three years for the development of prototypes of a lunar exploration rover, a Mars science rover, space robotics systems and technologies for in-orbit servicing. Total Canadian space sector revenues amounted in 2009 to CAD 2.8 billion, an increase of 8.2% from 2008 (nearly CAD 229 million), with satellite communications generating the largest share (Figure 19.2). Some 6 742 skilled workers are employed in the sector, including 3 242 highly qualified personnel. Ontario and Quebec have most of the space industry's workforce. Exports play a key role in revenue generation, as shown by the Canadian space sector's revenue breakdown with 50% coming from exports (Figure 19.3). The two main Canadian customers are the United States and Europe (Figure 19.4). The much larger Canadian aerospace industry comprises more than 400 firms located in every region of the country (AIAC, 2010). Collectively, these aerospace companies employ more than 80 000 employees. Since 1990, Canadian aerospace industry's sales have more than doubled, reaching CAD 23.6 billion in 2008, with more than 80% in exports. According to the *OECD International Trade by Commodity Statistics Database*, the positive trade balance for Canadian aerospace represented some USD 4 billion in 2009 (OECD, 2010).

Methodological notes

The Treasury Board of Canada provides an official annual report on Canadian plans and priorities, which takes into account the most recent budgetary measures. The Canadian Space Agency conducts annual industry surveys sent to some 200 organisations (including private entities, research organisations and universities) with strategic interests in the space industry, while the Aerospace Industries Association of Canada reports and aggregates data from the different provincial industry associations. Differing industry surveying methods may account for difference in data.

Sources

Aerospace Industries Association of Canada (AIAC) (2010), *AIAC Guide to Canada's Aerospace Industry 2010-2011*, Ottawa.

Canadian Space Agency (CSA) (2010), *State of the Canadian Space Sector 2010*, September.

OECD (2010), *OECD International Trade by Commodity Statistics Database*, OECD Publishing, Paris, August.

Treasury Board of Canada (2010), *Reports on Plans and Priorities (RPP): The Canadian Space Agency 2010-11*, Ottawa.

V. NATIONAL SPOTLIGHTS ON SELECTED COUNTRIES

19. Canada

19.1 Canadian space budget and distribution, 2009-13

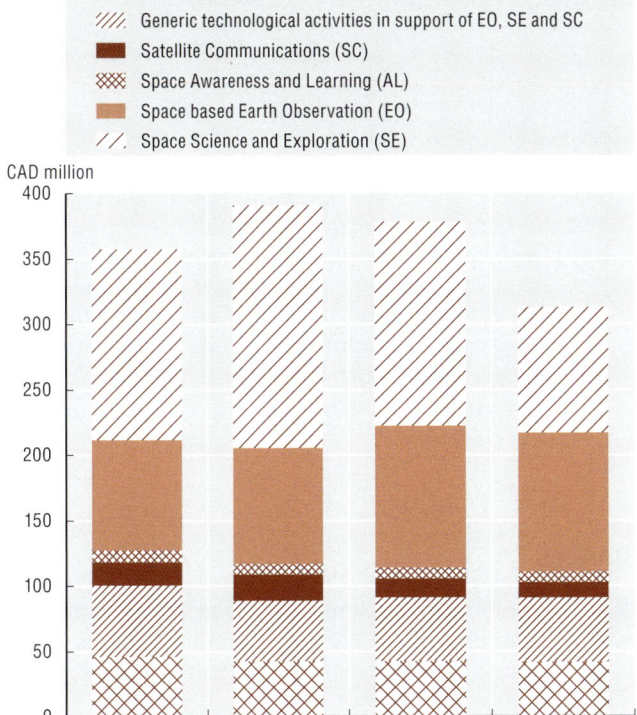

Source: Treasury Board of Canada (2010).

19.2 Canadian space sector revenues by activity sector and employment, 1996-2009

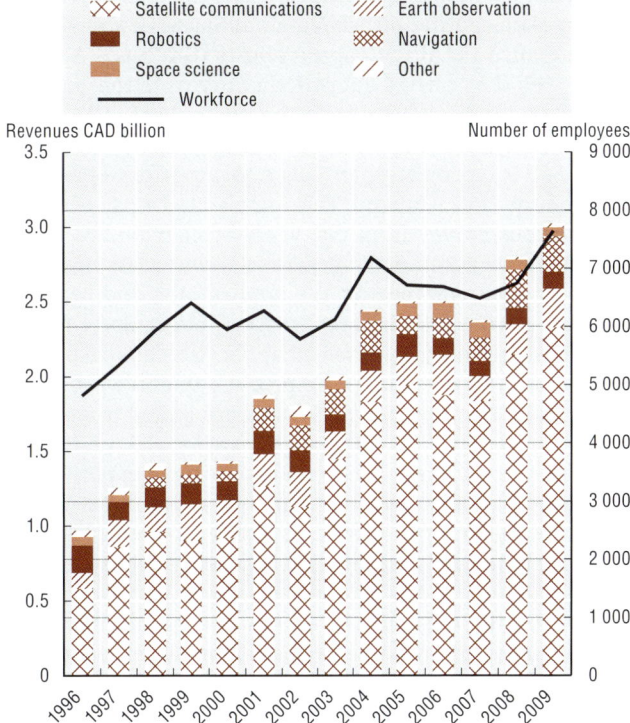

Source: CSA (2010).

19.3 Breakdown of Canadian space sector revenues (domestic versus exports), 1996-2009

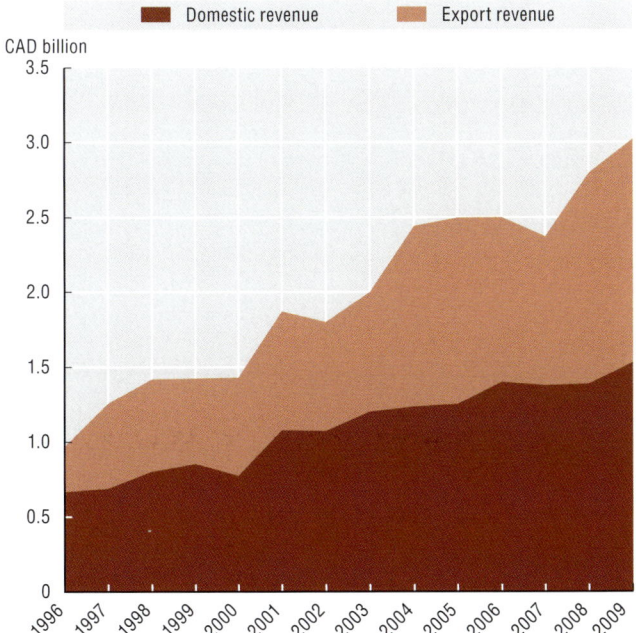

Source: CSA (2010).

19.4 Canadian space sector's export revenue by destination, 1996-2009

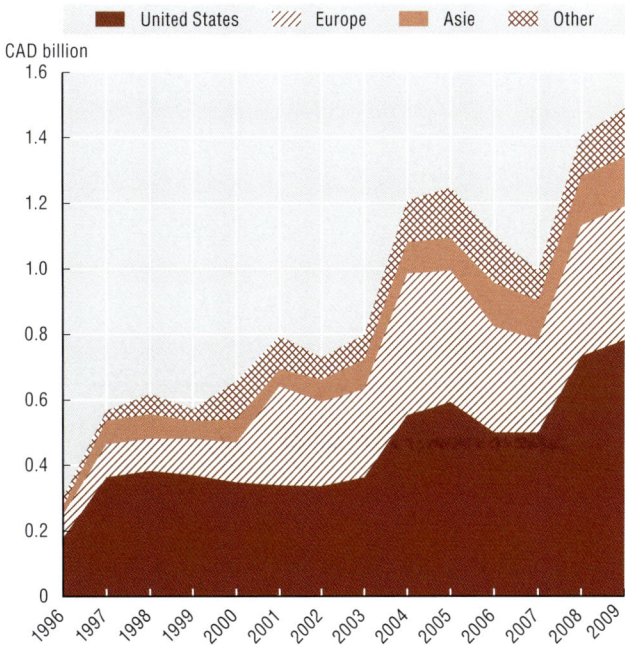

Source: CSA (2010).

THE SPACE ECONOMY AT A GLANCE 2011 © OECD 2011

V. NATIONAL SPOTLIGHTS ON SELECTED COUNTRIES

20. United Kingdom

The space budget for the United Kingdom amounted to GBP 312.52 million in 2010 (around USD 487.3 million). Around 13% is devoted to national programmes (GBP 41.34 million) (Figure 20.1). In April 2010, the UK Space Agency replaced the British National Space Centre (BNSC) to rationalise the British space efforts (UK Space Agency, 2010). BNSC has carried out periodic surveys of the size and health of the UK space industry since 1991. The most recent study, in 2010, found that the industry employed around 19 000 people, generating a turnover of GBP 5.8 billion (around USD 9 billion). This represented a rise of 8% on the previous survey from two years ago (Figure 20.2). The largest area of commercial growth in recent years has been in the downstream sector: the applications and services that use space. Satellite broadcasting, particularly television, is the primary commercial application of space technology, with sales of more than GBP 5 billion in 2008-09. The bulk of the remaining revenues are linked to applications for telecommunications, generating GBP 1.8 billion. Together these two applications account for over 90% of the space applications' revenues. Upstream and downstream industries have both grown at a rate of over 12%. The primary challenge is the lack of competent engineers in the market, as nearly 12% of the businesses survey respondents reported difficulty in filling their requirements. A major cluster of space activities in the UK is located in Harwell, Oxfordshire. It includes a new European Space Agency research facility (focusing on climate change modelling, innovative robotics systems and the design of new power sources), industries (Astrium, SSTL, Infoterra, Vega and Logica) the UK Space Agency, the Science Technology Facilities Council, Technology Strategy Board, Natural Environment Research Council and the South East England Development Agency (SEEDA).

Methodological notes

The budget figures are based on interim estimates, and the Ministry of Defence's expenditures on satellite telecommunications are not released publicly. The UK industry report produced for the UK Space Agency surveyed 260 companies across both upstream segments (companies which provide space technology) and downstream segments (companies that utilise space technologies).

Sources

Department for Business, Innovation and Skills (2010), "The Space Economy in the UK: An Economic Analysis of the Sector and the Role of Policy", *BIS Economics Paper*, No. 3, London, February.

UK Space Agency (UKSA) (2010a), "UK in Space 2010", *Annual Report*, Swindon, Wiltshire, July.

UKSA (2010b), *The Size and Health of the UK Space Industry*, Swindon, Wiltshire, November.

V. NATIONAL SPOTLIGHTS ON SELECTED COUNTRIES

20. United Kingdom

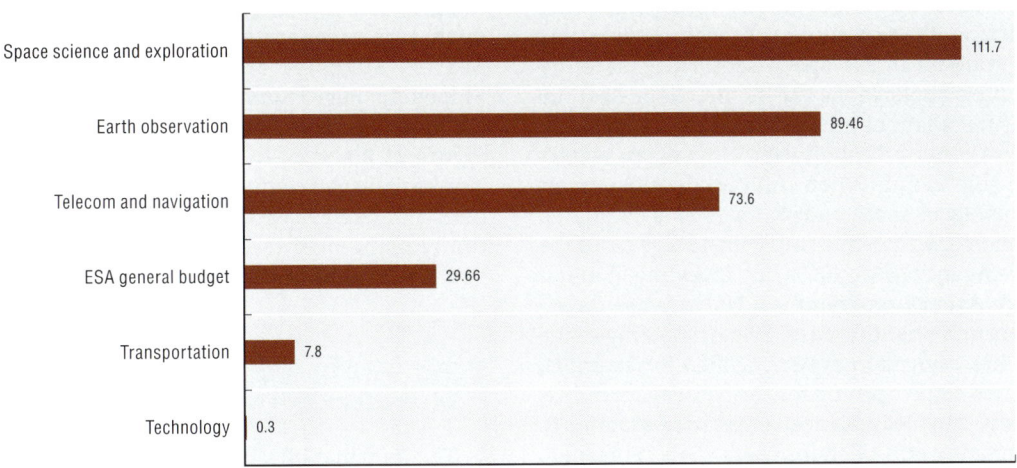

20.1 Distribution of UK space budget in 2010
GBP million (total budget GBP 312.52 million)

- Space science and exploration: 111.7
- Earth observation: 89.46
- Telecom and navigation: 73.6
- ESA general budget: 29.66
- Transportation: 7.8
- Technology: 0.3

Source: UKSA (2010a).

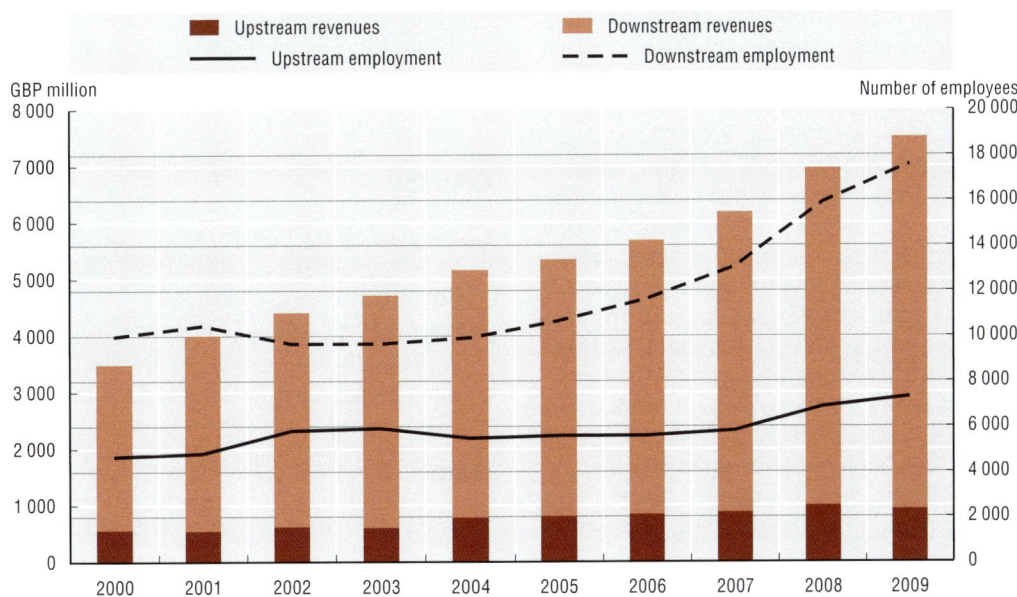

20.2 Revenues and employment in the UK space sector

Source: UKSA (2010b).

V. NATIONAL SPOTLIGHTS ON SELECTED COUNTRIES

21. Norway

Norway has been steadily developing its own space programme since setting up the Norwegian Space Centre (NSC) in 1987. Based on its geography and its specific national requirements, Norway is successfully pursuing several niche markets in the space sector (*e.g.* satellite telecommunication applications for its merchant fleet, oil and natural gas installations and the Svalbard archipelago; radar satellite services for monitoring Norwegian waters and automatic ship identification (AIS) to identify vessels at sea). The Norwegian space budget for 2009 is estimated at NOK 791 million (USD 125 million), with 46% going to the European Space Agency (NSC, 2010a). By investing in major European Space Agency programmes, Norway has developed its industry and scientific base. By participating in the European satellite navigation system Galileo for example, new opportunities could open up for the Norwegian industry, which already provides advanced navigation systems to professional shipping and offshore users. This represents an investment of about NOK 600 million until 2013 (NSC, 2010b). Recent national R&D programmes have also led to new applications, such as the combined use of the Norwegian satellite AISSat-1's AIS data with radar imagery, to monitor Norwegian waters. The Norwegian AISSat-1 was launched in July 2010. There are approximately 40 Norwegian companies and institutes involved in space activities. The total turnover of Norwegian space-related products and services was NOK 5.6 billion in 2009 (around USD 0.9 billion), an increase of 14% over 2008 (Figure 21.1). The export share represents some 72%, and the industry expects more growth in the years to come, despite the current economic crisis and the risks linked to fluctuations in USD and EUR exchange rates. The industry development seems to have slowed down around 2005, but this is mainly linked to the acquisition by foreign competitors of a number of Norwegian space players (*i.e.* Nera Satcom, Tandberg Television). This development shows the financial attractiveness of many Norwegian space actors, but also the challenge of keeping successful companies as national champions. The dominant Norwegian commercial activity concerns the sale of telecommunications and satellite broadcasting equipment and services, with actors such as Vizada Norway, Telenor, Norspace and STM Norway. But the development of ground stations, satellite imagery and other equipment involves many other actors, such as Kongsberg Gruppen (Defence and Aerospace, Seatex, Spacetec and Kongsberg Satellite Services), Shipequip, Fugro Survey, Fugro Seastar, Maritime Communications Partners Jotron Electronics and Blom Geomatics. Figure 21.2 shows the "spin-off effect" benefitting the Norwegian space industry. The amount of sales that are not directly linked to ESA or NSC contracts has been consistently rising over the past thirteen years to a coefficient of 4.7 in 2009, with the trend forecast to continue into 2013.

Methodological notes

The information is based on data from the Norwegian Space Centre and the Norwegian space industry. Values are in Norwegian kroner (NOK). The "spin-off effects" factor, indicating the coefficient by which ESA and NSC contracts lead to further sales by space-companies, is obtained by examining the relation between ESA/NSC contract activity and current/future business activities using a three-year time lag.

Sources

Norwegian Space Centre (NSC) (2010a), *Norges langtidsplan for romvirksomhet Handlingsplan, 2010-2013*, Oslo, June (in Norwegian).

NSC (2010b), *Norsk industri og-ESA deltakelse: Evaluering av industrielle ringvirkninger av Norsk deltakelse I ESA-samarbeidet, Norsk Romsenter*, Oslo, March (in Norwegian).

Notes

21.1 and 21.2: Actual and projected (2010, 2011, 2012, 2013).

V. NATIONAL SPOTLIGHTS ON SELECTED COUNTRIES

21. Norway

21.1 Turnover of Norwegian space-related goods and services from 1997 to 2013
Current prices in NOK

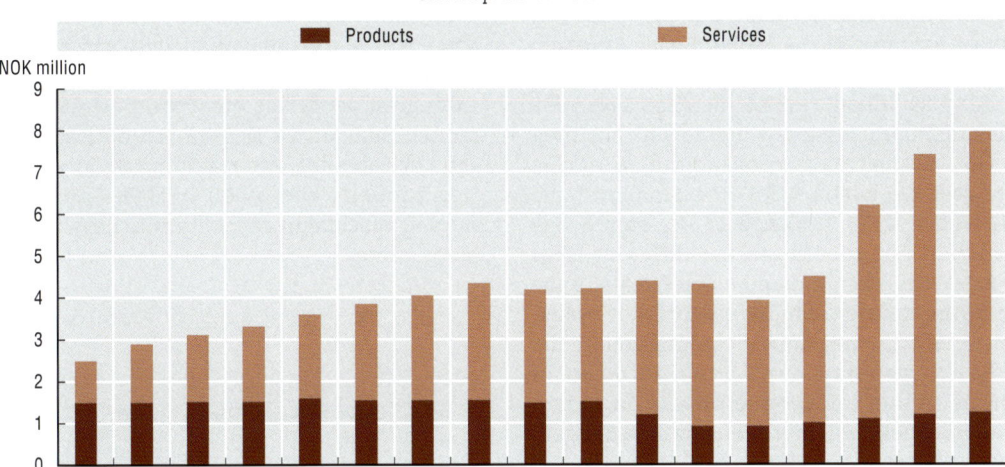

Source: NSC (2010a).

21.2 Spin-off factor for Norwegian ESA and Norwegian Space Centre Contracts, 1997-2013

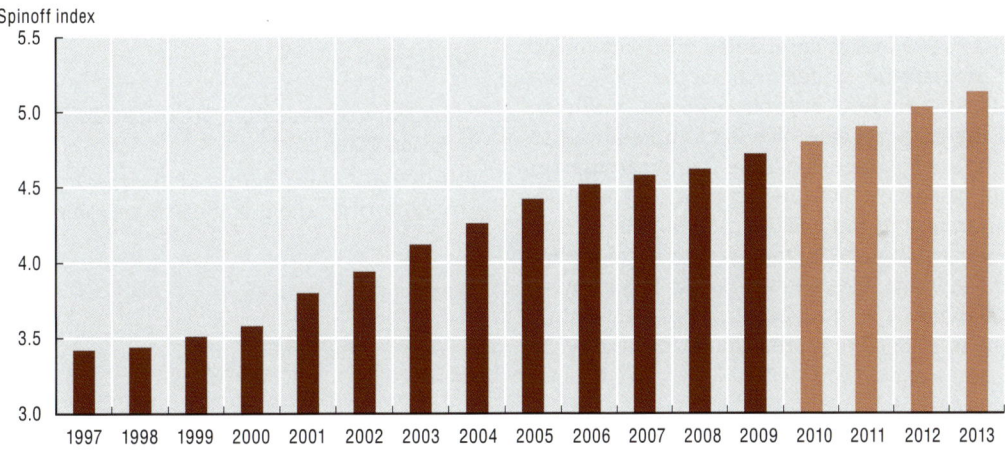

Source: NSC (2010b).

THE SPACE ECONOMY AT A GLANCE 2011 © OECD 2011

V. NATIONAL SPOTLIGHTS ON SELECTED COUNTRIES

22. India

India has one of the world's most ambitious space programmes, aiming to develop independent strategic capabilities, high technologies and a skilled Indian workforce. In 2010, the budget estimate of the Indian Space Research Organization (ISRO) reached a high of 57.78 billion Indian rupees (INR) (USD 1.24 billion), a 38% increase over 2009 (Figure 22.1). This rapid progression is in line with the five-year plan for the Indian space programme, which is expected to total INR 220 billion (USD 4.7 billion) over the 2007-12 period (Figure 22.2). ISRO has 14 782 employees (19.34% women) distributed between the different ISRO centres (Figure 22.3). The main Indian launch facility is the Satish Dhawan Space Centre, Sriharikota, which is also a major ISRO centre. Antrix, the commercial division of the Indian space agency, generates an annual turnover of USD 200 million by selling transponder leases on Indian telecommunications satellites, remote sensing data imagery (i.e. 20% of the global satellite imaging business), ground station services, satellite launches and exports of satellite components and other products. In July 2010, India launched commercially its 25th foreign satellite into orbit. The rising technological and manufacturing capabilities of the Indian aerospace industry, which now cover all segments in the industry (e.g. civil and military aviation, missiles) contribute to a larger share of commercial activities in the Indian space sector. Nearly 500 Indian companies take part in the national space programme, undertaking some 70% of the work on developing current launch vehicles, while in general 25% of the work on satellites is contracted out to industries. Aerospace companies can be found throughout India, with main clusters located in Bangalore, Hyderabad, Thiruvananthapuram and Sriharikota. Some benefit from the Special Economic Zones (SEZs) format with fiscal advantages to facilitate foreign direct investments. The number and diversity of Indian space missions keeps increasing: from 26 missions in 2002-07 to more than 50 in the 2007-12 period. India has one the largest domestic communication satellite systems, with eleven satellites providing a variety of communication services, including television coverage to some 90% of the population, with extensive use of telemedicine and tele-education in rural areas (see Chapter IV for examples). India has one spaceport with two independent launch pads and a fleet of ten optical and radar remote-sensing satellites. After sending a successful space exploration probe to the moon in 2008, India is investing into human spaceflight capabilities to develop its own astronaut programme.

Methodological notes

The budget figures use the Indian rupee (INR) as currency. In official Indian documents, the Rupee amounts are often given in Crores, a unit which corresponds to INR 10 million.

Sources

Indian Space Research Organization (ISRO) (2010), *Annual Report 2009-2010*.

Planning Commission of India (2010), *Five Year Plan (2007-2012)*, and previous, *http://planningcommission.gov.in*.

Note

22.1: 2010-11 estimates.

V. NATIONAL SPOTLIGHTS ON SELECTED COUNTRIES

22. India

22.1 India's space budget in 2010-11

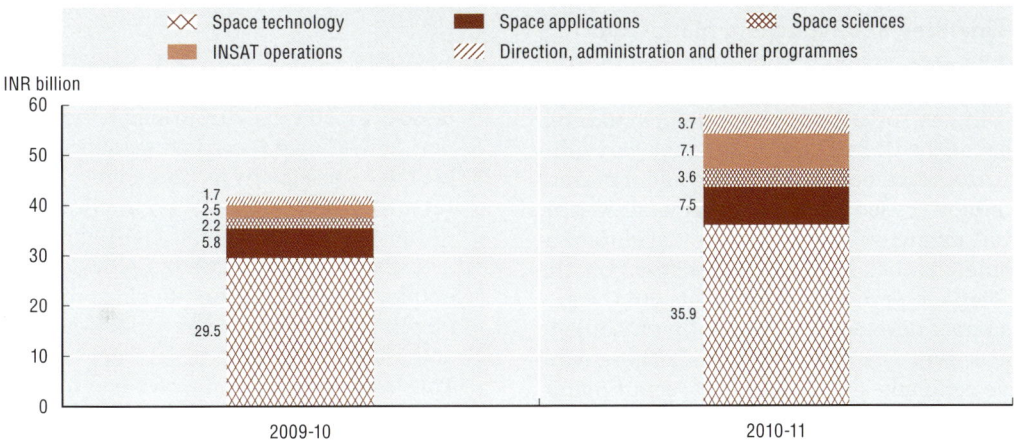

Source: ISRO (2010).

22.2 India's 5-year budget plans for space (from 1974 to 2012)

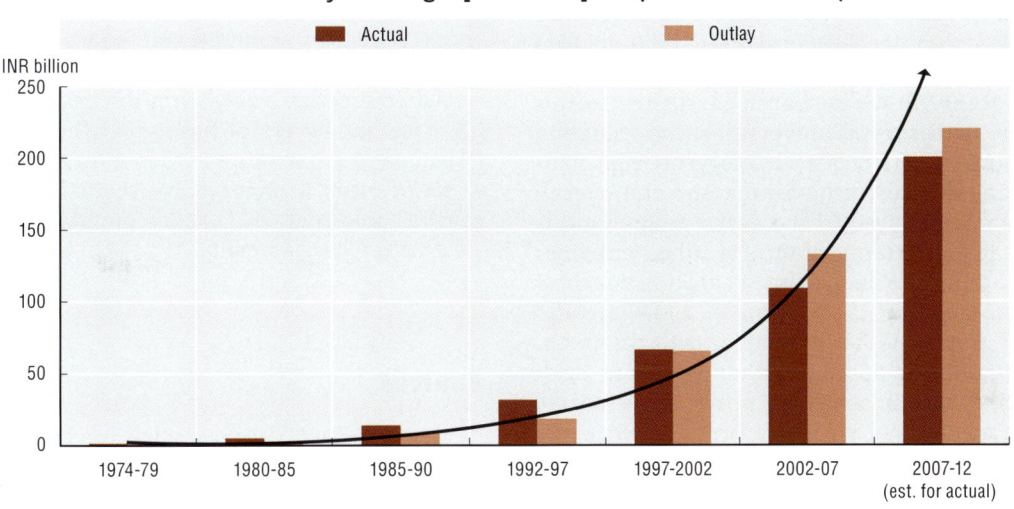

Source: Planning Commission of India (2010).

22.3 Employment in ISRO in 2010

Number of employees (total: 14 782 employees)

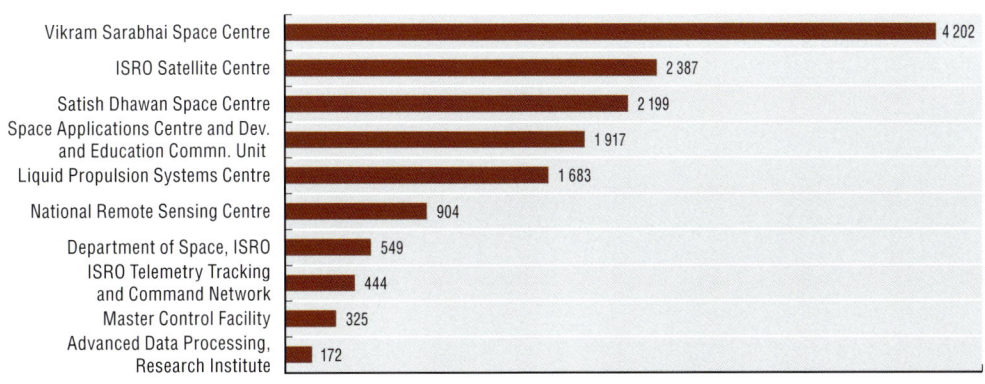

Source: ISRO (2010).

V. NATIONAL SPOTLIGHTS ON SELECTED COUNTRIES

23. China

China launched its first satellite in 1970 and has become a full blown space power, involved in every type of space activities (i.e. satellites and launchers manufacturing, spaceports, dedicated science and applications programmes, human spaceflight, military space). In 2010, China launched fifteen rockets carrying satellites to orbit, the same number as the United States. Although very difficult to estimate, the space budget for 2010 could represent some USD 6.5 billion, based on ongoing large-scale R&D programmes and extensive infrastructure development (e.g. a fourth Chinese launch site is under construction, the Chang'e 2 satellite is to orbit the Moon in late 2011, and a space station is under development, with a first module to be placed in orbit over the next two years). There were some 40 Chinese companies involved in spacecraft manufacturing in 2009, including joint ventures, commercial and state-owned enterprises. These companies represent around 48 000 people directly employed in the space sector in China, out of more than 500 000 people employed in the larger aerospace sector, an integral part of the defence industry. As noted in OECD (2008), the restructuring of commercial and state-owned companies since the mid-1990s has downsized several industrial sectors including aerospace, but has also enhanced productivity (Figure 23.1). Many public research institutes, often defence-related, and several universities (e.g. Tsinghua University, Beijing University of Technology) are contributing to the Chinese space programme and the overall Chinese workforce involved in the space programme is probably much larger. In terms of turnover, the companies surveyed by the Chinese National Bureau of Statistics show revenues of some CNY 140 billion in 2009 (around USD 20 billion), a value rather consistent with the intensiveness of the Chinese space programme (Figure 23.2). Major companies active in aerospace activities are located throughout China, particularly in the regions of Shaanxi, Jiangsu, Sichuan, Guizhou, Liaoning, Shanghai and Beijing, with a concentration of aerospace industry in the Eastern part of the country (Figure 23.3).

Methodological notes

The data come from OECD calculations, based on statistics from the Chinese National Bureau of Statistics (2009 and 2010). China's Industrial Classification for National Economic Activities (CSIC, Rev. 2002) includes subsections for aeronautics and space manufacturing. Both sectors are included in the larger Chinese Defence industry. Official data about the aerospace and space sectors provide only a glance at employment and revenues, since most research and development activities – particularly for space activities – take place in military enterprise groups. This overlap between the civil and the military, which can also be found in OECD countries, adds complexity to the analysis. Using annual surveys, the Chinese National Bureau of Statistics classifies companies according to the original value of their productive fixed assets. In the case of the space industry (mainly assembly plants): large-sized companies (CNY 70 million and above), medium-sized companies (CNY 30 to 70 million), and small-sized companies (under CNY 30 million), are included in the "commercial enterprises" category in the figures. The Chinese space budget is not based on official data, but on estimates to provide an order of magnitude (i.e. analysis of other R&D intensive sectors, experiences in OECD and non-OECD space programmes and infrastructure development).

Sources

OECD (2008), *OECD Reviews of Innovation Policy: China*, OECD Publishing, Paris.

OECD calculations based on data from the Chinese National Bureau of Statistics (2009, 2010), *China Statistics Yearbook on High Technology Industry*, Beijing, December.

V. NATIONAL SPOTLIGHTS ON SELECTED COUNTRIES

23. China

23.1 Number of Chinese firms and workforce involved in spacecraft manufacturing (1995-2009)

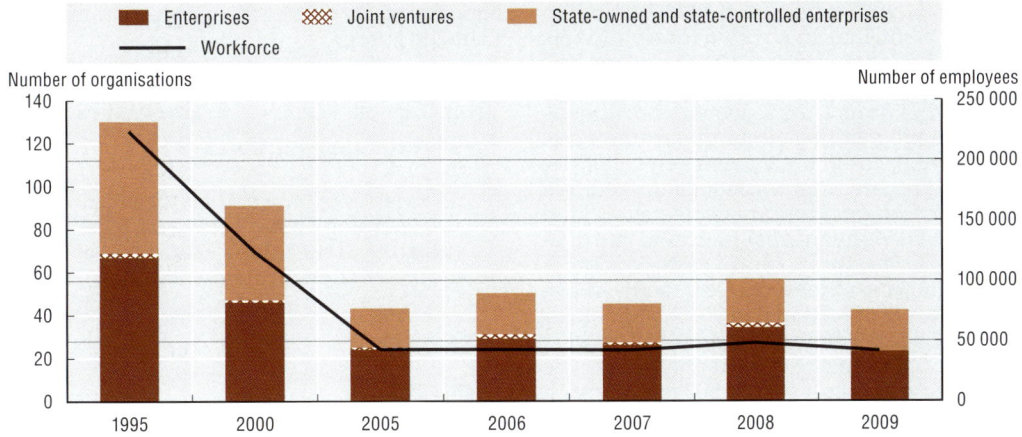

23.2 Revenues of Chinese companies involved in spacecraft manufacturing, 1995-2008

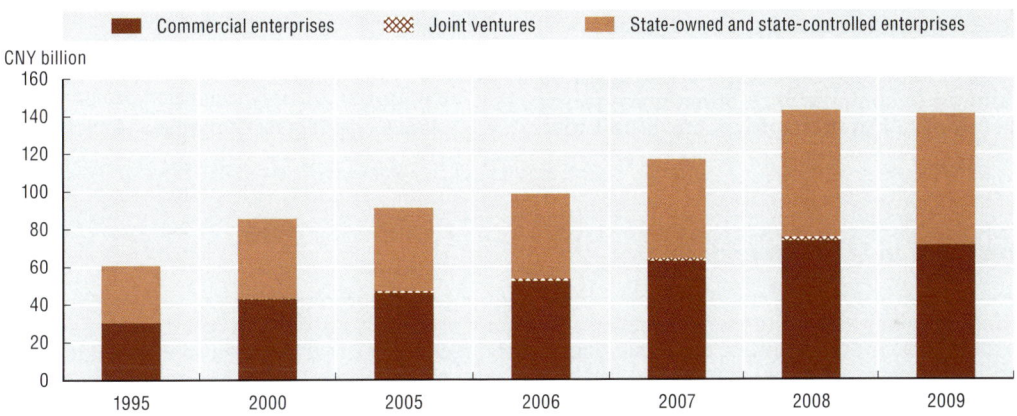

23.3 Chinese regions with aerospace industry

Number of employees and number of commercial aerospace companies

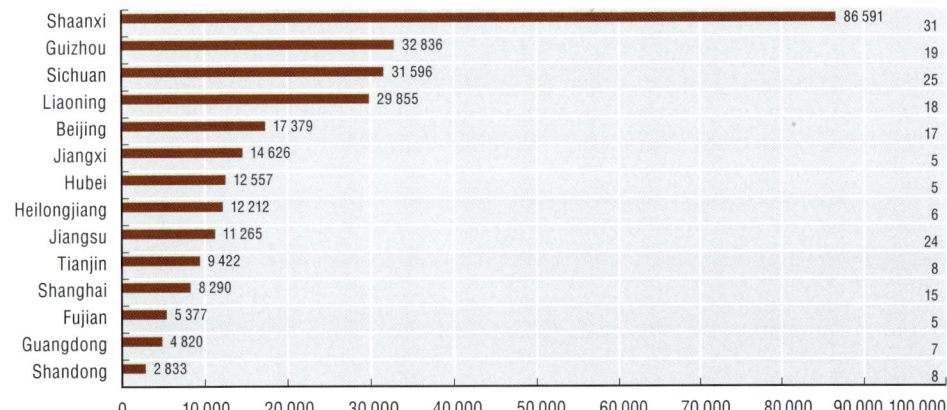

Region	Employees	Companies
Shaanxi	86 591	31
Guizhou	32 836	19
Sichuan	31 596	25
Liaoning	29 855	18
Beijing	17 379	17
Jiangxi	14 626	5
Hubei	12 557	5
Heilongjiang	12 212	6
Jiangsu	11 265	24
Tianjin	9 422	8
Shanghai	8 290	15
Fujian	5 377	5
Guangdong	4 820	7
Shandong	2 833	8

V. NATIONAL SPOTLIGHTS ON SELECTED COUNTRIES

24. Brazil

Brazil's space programme covers the entire range of space technologies and applications. The Brazilian space agency (Agência Espacial Brasileira, AEB) is the largest space organisation in Latin America, with a budget of BRL 352 million in 2010 (around USD 210 million). In co-ordination with AEB, the National Institute for Space Research (INPE) designs half of Brazilian satellite subsystems and contracts them to the industry. It is estimated that some 3 400 people work directly for the Brazilian space programme, either in governmental agencies or industry (AEB, 2010). Brazil owns ten satellites, the majority procured for telecommunications. In addition to meteorology, some of its satellites are dedicated to land remote sensing, and have been designed and built in co-operation with China. The China – Brazil Earth Resources Satellites (CBERS) programme so far includes a family of five remote-sensing satellites (2 operational in 2010) built jointly by Brazil and China. CBERS-3 should be launched in 2011 and CBERS-4 in 2014. The Brazilian participation in the programme amounts to a total cost of USD 500 million, with 60% of investment taking the form of industrial contracts. From 2004 to 2010, more than 1.5 million images were delivered to users in Brazil, Latin America and China for forestry and agriculture assessment (e.g. sugarcane and soybean crops assessments), urban management and geological mapping. From 2012 onwards, African ground stations in South Africa, the Canary Islands, Egypt and Gabon will receive and freely share CBERS data. The country is developing indigenous rocket launching capabilities at its Alcantara Space Centre, aiming to compete with other space-faring countries in commercial launch provision. Brazil also contributes data from its own meteorological satellite to the World Meteorological Organisation and should join the European Southern Observatory (ESO) organisation in 2011, becoming its fifteenth member state and the first from outside Europe.

Methodological notes

The data are provided by the Brazilian space agency, the Planning Commission and the Brazilian aerospace industry association. All figures are in the national currency, the Brazilian real (BRL).

Sources

Associação das Indústrias Aeroespaciais do Brasil (AIAB) (2009), *Números da Associação das Indústrias Aeroespaciais do Brasil*, Brasilia, Brazil, www.aiab.org.br.

Brazilian Space Agency (EAB) (2011), *Annual Report*, Brasilia, Brazil.

Comissão Mista De Planos, Orçamentos Públicos E Fiscalização (2010), *Despesas por projeto/atividade/operação especial – por órgão*, Congresso Nacional (in Brazilian).

Space programmes in Latin America

Many countries in Latin America are developing their own space programmes. Brazil and Mexico are the largest owners and operators of space systems in the region, but many other Latin American countries are actively seeking to develop their own space programmes. Micro-satellites are currently being developed in Argentina, Chile and Peru, while international astronomical telescope facilities have been established in Chile, Colombia, Honduras, Paraguay, Peru and Uruguay. A number of countries also have their own astronauts, who flew to orbit using the US Space Shuttle or the Russian Soyuz system.

- **Argentina:** The Comision Nacional de Actividades Espaciales (CONAE) is the country's space agency, which has already designed some small satellites. Owner of five procured telecommunications satellites, Argentina is starting to build its own satellites: ARSAT-1, the first geostationary communications satellite is planned to be launched in 2011. The country is also pursuing new remote sensing capabilities.
- **Chile:** Chile became the 31st member of the OECD in 2010. It has recently formed a space agency (Agencia Chilena Espacio – ACE) and is developing remote sensing and micro-satellite capabilities. It aims to launch its first earth observation satellite (dubbed Sistema Satelital para Observación de la Tierra) by 2011. The country's geographic location has also allowed the development of national scientific space research programmes, particularly in astronomy, with the setting up of several large international telescopes.
- **Colombia:** The Colombian Space Commission was created in 2006 to promote the development of space activities, particularly remote sensing applications.
- **Ecuador:** The Ecuadorian Civilian Space Agency (Agencia Espacial Civil Ecuatoriana EXA) was established in November 2007. An active suborbital programme is underway with the objective to fly microgravity experiments and future astronauts.
- **Mexico:** Mexico, an OECD member state since 1994, has focused on developing commercial satellite communication services. In 1997, the Mexican government created the Satelites Mexicanos (Satmex) to oversee its satellite operations and the company currently owns three satellites in orbit. The national space agency (Agencia Espacial Mexicana, AEXA) was created in 2010, as a decentralised public agency responsible for encouraging the development of scientific and technological research.
- **Peru:** Peru is developing remote sensing capabilities, particularly to tackle natural disasters, via its National Aerospace Research and Development Commission (Comisión Nacional de Investigación y Desarrollo Aeroespacial – CONIDA). The objectives are to launch a sounding rocket and a mini-satellite, as well as forming and training the first Peruvian astronaut.
- **Uruguay:** The Aeronautics and Space Research and Dissemination Centre (Centro de Investigación y Difusión Aeronáutico-Espacial – CIDAE) is in charge of co-ordinating international co-operation, particularly for astronomy.

V. NATIONAL SPOTLIGHTS ON SELECTED COUNTRIES

24. Brazil

24.1 Key statistics on the Brazillian aerospace sector, 2005-08

	2005	2006	2007	2008
Revenues (USD billion)	4.3	4.3	6.2	7.55
Share of GDP (%)	1.5	1.5	1.9	2.02
Exports (USD billion)	3.7	3.9	5.6	6.74
Employment	19.800	22.000	25.200	27.100
Main sectors				
Aeronautics (%)	87.3	90.8	91.3	89.13
Defence (%)	9.29	5.78	6.6	8.79
Space (%)	0.24	0.41	0.4	0.57
Total exports as a % of revenues	**90**	**90.5**	**90.8**	**90.8**

Source: AIAB (2009).

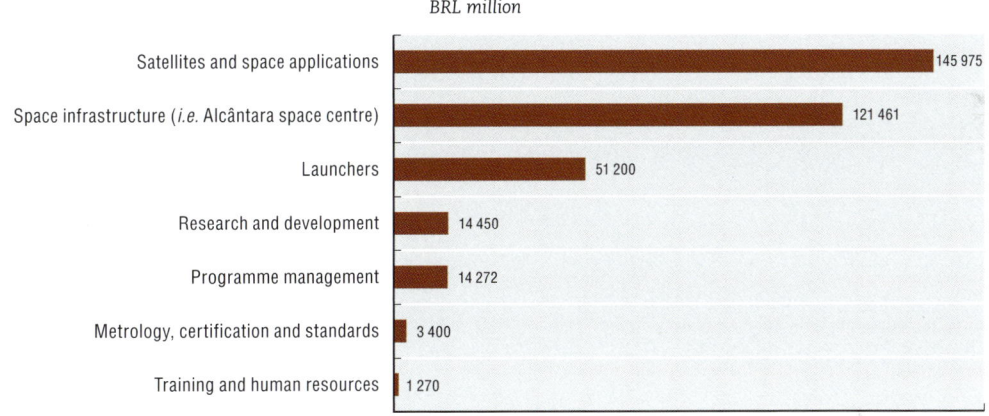

24.2 Brazilian space budget distribution, 2010

Source: Comissão Mista De Planos (2010).

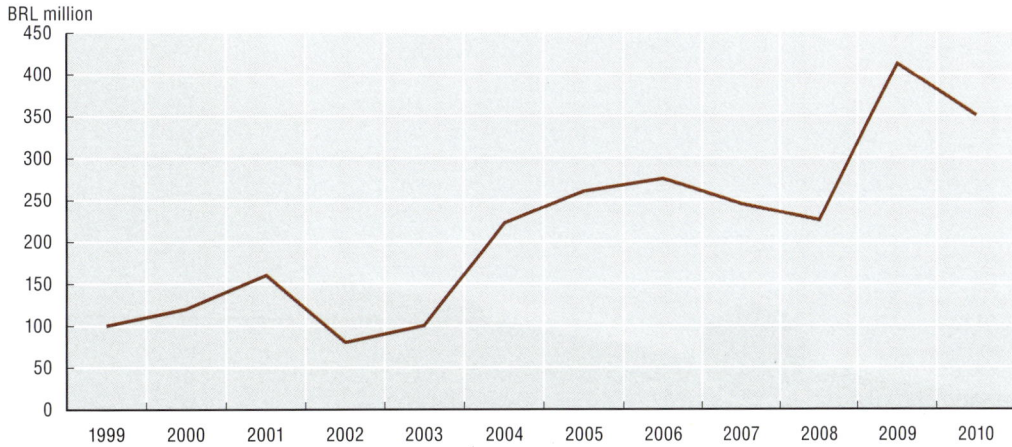

24.3 Brazilian space budget

Source: EAB (2011).

VI. THE GLOBAL AEROSPACE SECTOR IN PERSPECTIVE

25. Production and value-added

26. Research and development

27. Trade

This final chapter provides an overview of the global aerospace sector. The space economy evolved from the aerospace industry and the two still share many aspects, components and technologies (e.g. space launchers are modified guided-missiles). Detailed examination of the space sector is hampered by this legacy since many data are still classified according to categories defined for the wider aerospace. The following sections examine trends in aerospace production, research and development and trade.

VI. THE GLOBAL AEROSPACE SECTOR IN PERSPECTIVE

25. Production and value-added

A few countries dominate the global aerospace production in 2010, with major industry players being involved in both aeronautics and space systems (Table 25.2). The United States and European countries remain the prominent aerospace markets, with sales in the United States representing some USD 214 billion for 2009, followed by Europe, Canada and Japan. However, China, India, Mexico and Brazil are emerging as important customers of aerospace products. The aerospace sector is one of the fastest globalising industries in terms of both market structure and production system. In addition to satellite systems, new aeronautic markets are developing based on the growth in air traffic worldwide (expected to continue rising 4.9% on an annual basis over the next 10 years), and increases in military aerospace expenditures. Despite its strategic nature, aerospace represents a small percentage of the total manufacturing value added in G7 countries (Figure 25.4). The percentage for all G7 countries remains below 4% of the total in 2008 (Figure 25.3).

Methodological notes

Production represents the value of goods and/or services produced in a year, whether sold or stocked, while value added for an industry refers to its contribution to national Gross Domestic Product (GDP). It is often considered a better measure of output than basic production since it reduces the likelihood of double counting that is possible with the production approach. The data come from OECD's Structural Analysis Statistics (STAN) database, which includes statistics for most OECD countries. To make the values comparable, Purchasing Power Parities were used to convert current production values into USD. Some care should be taken with the interpretation of Production since it includes intermediate inputs (such as energy, materials and services required to produce final output). Other data presented here come from private sources (aerospace industry associations) to illustrate recent trends nationally and regionally. As such, and due to industry associations' distinct methods in data definition, collection and analysis, as well as reporting in national currencies, international comparability is very limited.

Sources

DeCarlo (2010), *Forbes' 2000 Ranking*, www.forbes.com.

OECD (2010), "OECD Structural Analysis Statistics", STAN Industry Database, www.oecd.org/sti/stan.

Further reading

AeroSpace and Defence Industries Association (ASD), www.asd-europe.org.

Aerospace Industries Association of America (AIA), www.aia-aerospace.org.

Aerospace Industries Association of Canada (AIAC), www.aiac.ca.

French Aerospace Industries Association (GIFAS), www.gifas.asso.fr.

German Aerospace Industries Association (BDLI), www.bdli.de.

Japanese Aerospace Industries Association (SJAC), www.sjac.or.jp.

United Kingdom Aerospace, Defence and Security Group, www.adsgroup.org.uk.

VI. THE GLOBAL AEROSPACE SECTOR IN PERSPECTIVE

25. Production and value-added

25.1 Aerospace production as a share of national manufacturing production, 2008 or latest year

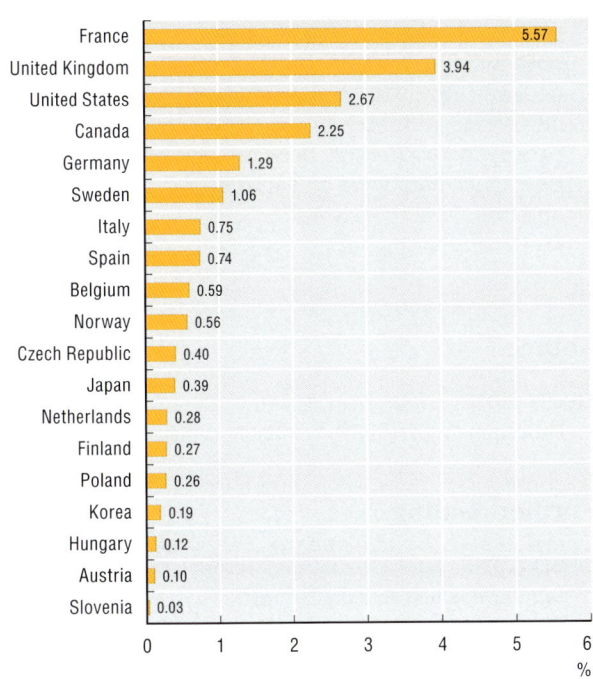

25.2 Aerospace and defense leading companies in 2010, in Forbe's ranking

Company		Sales (USD billion)	Profits (USD billion)	Assets (USD billion)	Market value (USD billion)	Space activities
Boeing	United States	68.28	1.31	62.05	48.45	Yes
EADS	Netherlands	61.44	−1.09	111.40	16.75	Yes
Lockheed Martin	United States	45.19	3.02	35.11	29.61	Yes
Northrop Grumman	United States	33.76	1.69	30.25	19.08	Yes
BAE Systems5	United Kingdom	32.91	−0.11	38.58	19.99	Yes
General Dynamics	United States	31.98	2.39	31.08	28.51	Yes
Raytheon	United States	24.88	1.94	23.61	21.53	Yes
Finmeccanica	Italy	20.94	0.80	40.69	7.49	Yes
Bombardier	Canada	19.44	0.81	22.12	9.68	No
Thales	France	17.96	−0.28	25.81	7.67	Yes
Rolls-Royce Group	United Kingdom	16.82	3.59	24.32	15.57	Yes
L-3 Communications	United States	15.62	0.90	14.81	10.62	Yes
Safran	France	14.72	0.89	26.04	9.32	Yes
SAIC	United States	10.68	0.49	5.41	7.72	Yes
Goodrich	United States	6.69	0.60	8.74	8.42	Yes
Precision Castparts	United States	5.65	0.94	7.46	16.46	No
Dassault Aviation	France	5.22	0.52	13.54	7.40	Yes
Embraer	Brazil	5.12	0.19	9.04	3.96	No
Rockwell Collins	United States	4.44	0.56	4.65	9.18	Yes
Singapore Technologies	Singapore	3.95	0.32	4.81	6.68	Yes
Cobham	United Kingdom	3.04	0.30	3.91	4.22	No

StatLink http://dx.doi.org/10.1787/888932400475

25.3 Aerospace value added as a share of the national manufacturing value added for G7 countries, 2008 or latest year

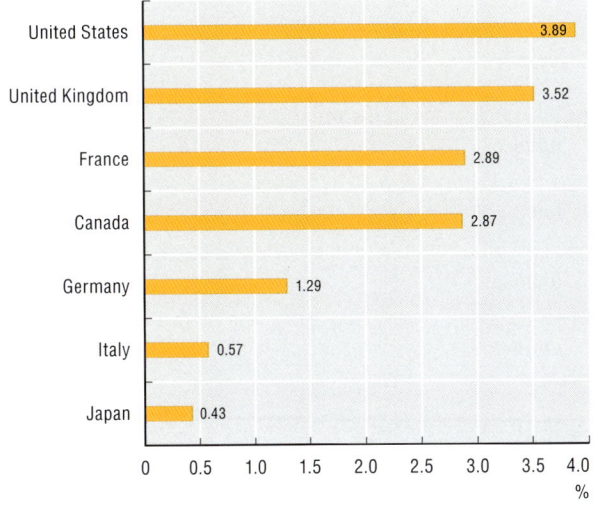

StatLink http://dx.doi.org/10.1787/888932400513

25.4 Value added by the aerospace industry for G7 countries, 2007 or latest year

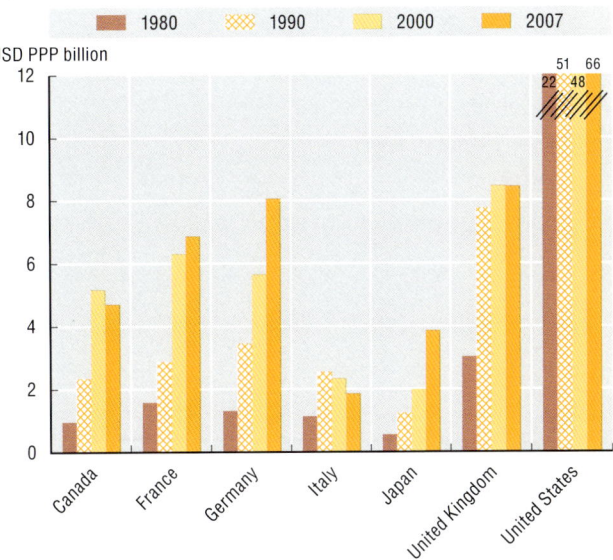

StatLink http://dx.doi.org/10.1787/888932400494

VI. THE GLOBAL AEROSPACE SECTOR IN PERSPECTIVE

26. Research and development

The official OECD statistics relating to aerospace industry research and development (R&D) presented here focus on business enterprise research and development (BERD) data. BERD is considered to be closely linked to the development of new products and production techniques. BERD data for aerospace are heavily dominated by a few large countries. Four of the OECD's largest industrial spenders – the United States, France, the United Kingdom and Germany – account for more than 80% of the total (Table 26.1). The evolution of BERD performed in the aerospace industry for selected OECD countries shows the industry in the United States investing twice as much as the total European industry. Taken nationally, the French, German and British aerospace industries invested each four times less than their American counterparts in 2006 (Figure 26.2).

Methodological notes

The OECD Analytical Business Enterprise Research and Development (ANBERD) database provides internationally comparable time-series on industrial R&D expenditures. The data on R&D expenditures by the aerospace industry are based on official statistics provided to the OECD by its member countries. Aerospace data were only available for selected OECD and non-OECD countries.

Source

OECD (2010), *Analytical Business Enterprise Research and Development (ANBERD) Database*, www.oecd.org/sti/anberd.

Further reading

OECD (2010), *Main Science and Technology Indicators (MSTI) Database*, www.oecd.org/sti/msti.

Notes

26.1: Non-OECD countries.

26.2: Europe: BERD budgets of Austria, Belgium, the Czech Republic, Finland, France, Germany, Greece, Ireland, Italy, the Netherlands, Norway, Poland, Spain and Sweden.

VI. THE GLOBAL AEROSPACE SECTOR IN PERSPECTIVE

26. Research and development

26.1 BERD performed in the aerospace industry for selected OECD and non-OECD countries 2008 or latest year

	BERD performed in aerospace (current USD PPP million)	Percentage of BERD performed in the aerospace industry
Australia	81.515	0.91
Austria	19.465	0.34
Belgium	95.713	1.91
Canada	780.558	6.14
Czech Republic	48.077	1.964
Finland	17.0134	0.354
France	2 995.318	10.80
Germany	2 246.780	4.33
Italy	1 230.306	10.62
Japan	427.401	0.40
Korea	36.306	0.11
Netherlands	0.1774	0.01
Norway	44.904	0.711
Poland	3.760	0.141
Spain	47.552	4.721
Sweden	396.490	3.871
United Kingdom	289.808	3.16
United States	3 209.661	13.24
Russian Federation	1 8436	6.84
Singapore	541.118	2.60

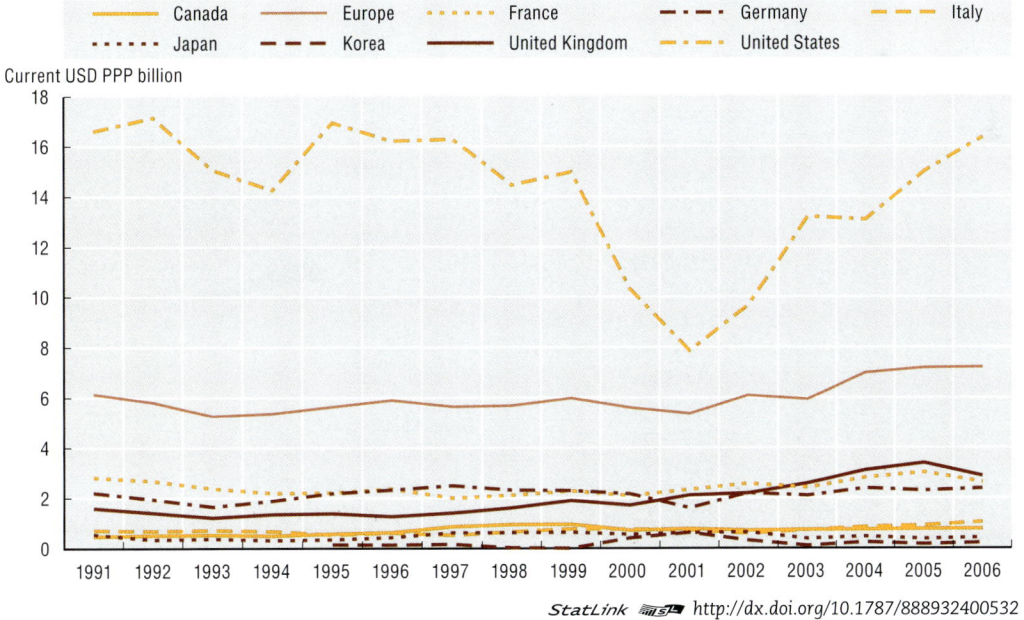

26.2 Evolution of BERD performed in the aerospace industry for selected OECD countries, 1991-2006

StatLink http://dx.doi.org/10.1787/888932400532

VI. THE GLOBAL AEROSPACE SECTOR IN PERSPECTIVE

27. Trade

OECD countries account for 90% of the total exports of aerospace products. As shown in Figure 27.3, sixteen countries show a positive aerospace trade balance in 2008, with the United States, France, Germany, Canada, Italy and the Russian Federation having the most revenues. China, Singapore and Japan are mainly importers of aerospace products and services, showing a negative trade balance. The 2009 data confirms that despite the economic crisis, the major aerospace countries have still exported large amounts of products (Table 27.1). Specialisation-wise, aerospace exports represent more than 30% of France, the Russian Federation and the United States' exports of high technologies (Figure 27.2). India, Japan and China do not rely as much on their aerospace exports, as they are more specialised in the exports of radio and television equipment (Japan and China) and pharmaceuticals (India).

Methodological notes

The data are extracted from the OECD STAN Database and the CPII Chelem Database. The ISIC category used is "C353 Aircraft and Spacecraft", which may not take into account some aerospace products and services found in other categories (*e.g.* military equipment). Trade data in all OECD countries are collected using the Harmonised System (HS) or some classification derived from it.

Sources

Centre d'Études Prospectives et d'Informations Internationales (CEPII) (2010), *Chelem Database*, www.cepii.fr.

OECD (2010), *OECD Structural Analysis Statistics (STAN) Industry Database*, www.oecd.org/sti/stan.

Note

27.1: Values only available for a number of OECD countries.

27.1 Aerospace trade balance for selected OECD countries in 2009

Current USD

	2009
United States	64 491 908 369
France	18 356 181 589
Germany	6 208 345 562
Canada	4 085 020 557
Italy	2 703 813 856
Australia	484 296 101
Belgium	420 440 895
Czech Republic	261 782 995
Mexico	156 215 228
Switzerland	127 237 283
Luxembourg	−5 766 161
Sweden	−85 604 818
Austria	−519 511 374
Turkey	−763 811 082
Finland	−815 139 295
Denmark	−1 174 356 738
Ireland	−4 288 805 398
United Kingdom	−4 544 263 091

27.2 Aerospace export market share for selected OECD and non-OECD countries in 2008

Percentage

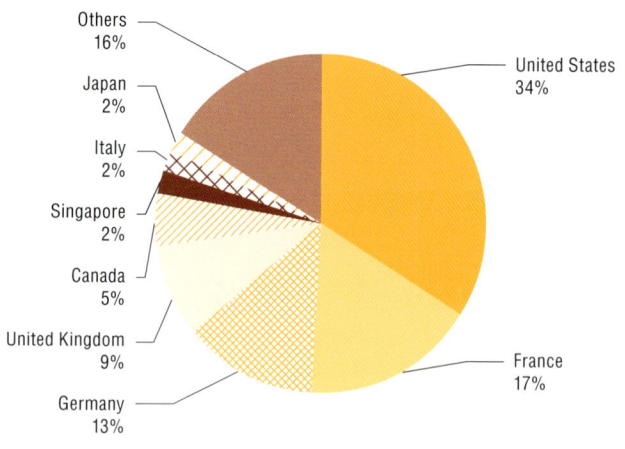

VI. THE GLOBAL AEROSPACE SECTOR IN PERSPECTIVE

27. Trade

27.3 Aerospace global export market share and trade balance for selected OECD and non-OECD countries in 2008

Export market share (percentage) and current USD million

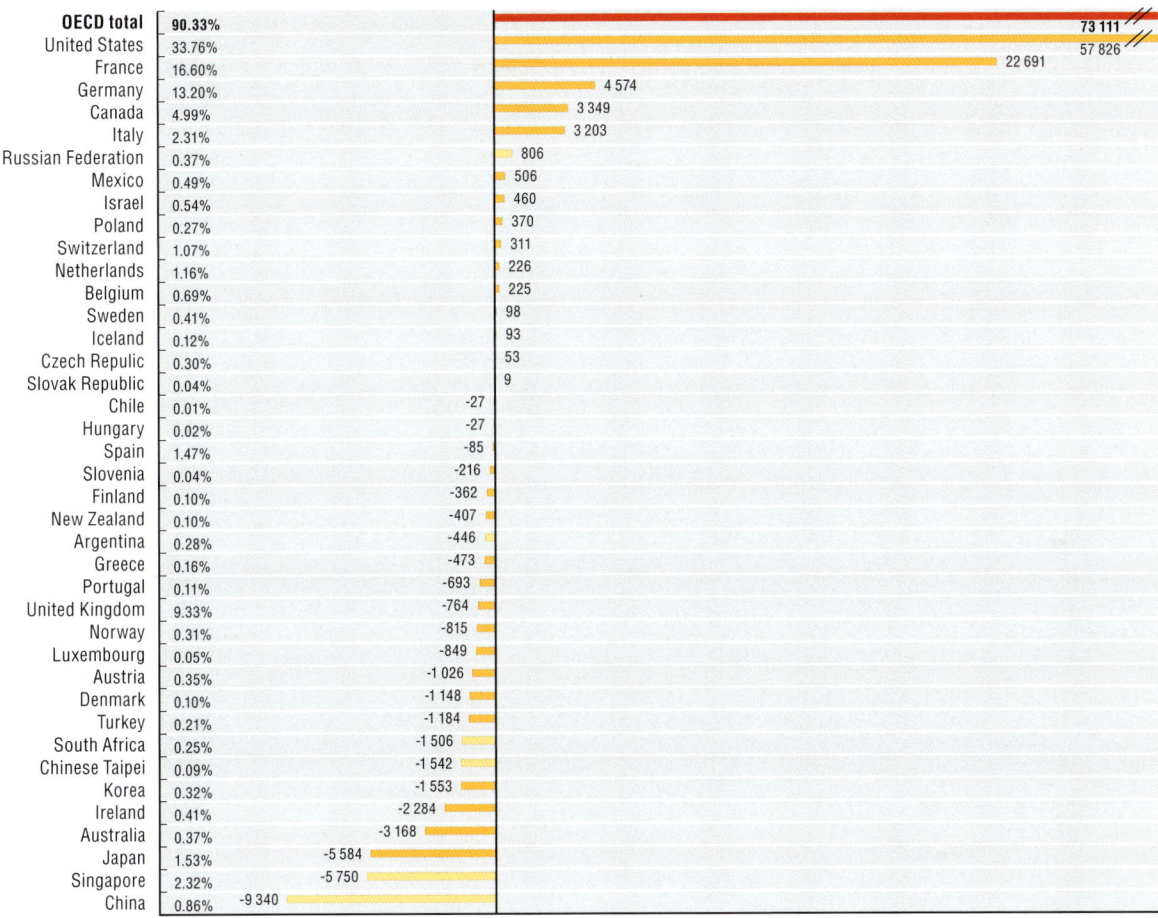

StatLink http://dx.doi.org/10.1787/888932400551

27.4 Exports of high-technology products, specialisation of selected countries in 2008

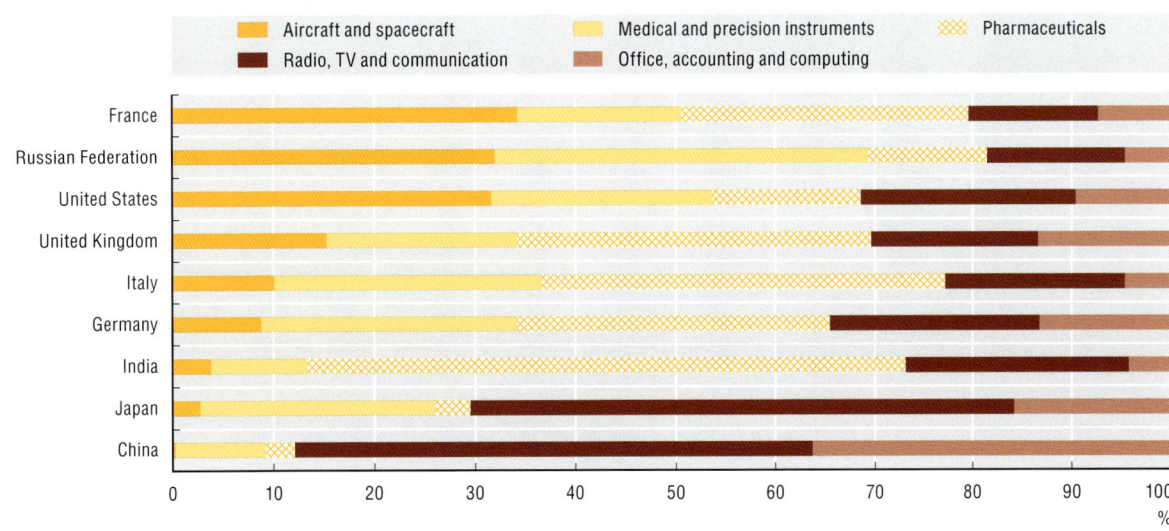

THE SPACE ECONOMY AT A GLANCE 2011 © OECD 2011

113

ORGANISATION FOR ECONOMIC CO-OPERATION AND DEVELOPMENT

The OECD is a unique forum where governments work together to address the economic, social and environmental challenges of globalisation. The OECD is also at the forefront of efforts to understand and to help governments respond to new developments and concerns, such as corporate governance, the information economy and the challenges of an ageing population. The Organisation provides a setting where governments can compare policy experiences, seek answers to common problems, identify good practice and work to co-ordinate domestic and international policies.

The OECD member countries are: Australia, Austria, Belgium, Canada, Chile, the Czech Republic, Denmark, Estonia, Finland, France, Germany, Greece, Hungary, Iceland, Ireland, Israel, Italy, Japan, Korea, Luxembourg, Mexico, the Netherlands, New Zealand, Norway, Poland, Portugal, the Slovak Republic, Slovenia, Spain, Sweden, Switzerland, Turkey, the United Kingdom and the United States. The European Union takes part in the work of the OECD.

OECD Publishing disseminates widely the results of the Organisation's statistics gathering and research on economic, social and environmental issues, as well as the conventions, guidelines and standards agreed by its members.